Adventures of a
WITNESS
for JESUS

Grace

52
true stories
show how God
empowers His
people...to
be witnesses!

By
G. Warren Sears

ISBN 978-0-9790221-2-8

All illustrations, including cover, by G. Warren Sears
All scripture is from the King James Version.
Some names have been changed to respect privacy.

Published by:
YAV Publications
Lutherville-Timonium, Maryland
YAV books may be purchased in bulk for educational,
business, fund-raising, or sales promotional use.
For information, please contact Books@yav.com
Visit our website: www.InterestingWriting.com

5 7 9 10 8 6 4

Printed in the United States of America
Printed on Recycled Paper
Published May 2008

TABLE OF CONTENTS

Part One: The Adventures

1. In the Big City

2. In the Marketplace

3. Strangers in the Street

4. Witnessing on the Job

5. Praise God in Public Meetings

6. Class Acts

7. In the Neighborhood

8. Confrontations

9. Hitchhikers

10. Visiting Jesus in Jail

Part Two: Helps

18. Testimonies

19. Gospel Tracts

Part Three: Final Answers

My Final Answer to:

Appendices

ACKNOWLEDGMENTS

Thank you, Lord Jesus, for making this book possible by putting so many wonderful people in my life that have prayed for me, helped me and encouraged me in countless ways, all for your glory. And special thanks to...

Dr. R. Herbert Fitzpatrick for many Sunday morning messages that stirred me up to be a witness;

Rev. Nathan Butler for invaluable lessons and examples in preaching the Gospel on the streets in the inner city;

Kay Campbell who gave me a terrific book—"The Writer's Companion" by Richard Marius;

Art Landerman for his help with the cover illustration;

Brenda and Frank Sears for their inexhaustible patience in teaching me to use the computer word processor and bringing me a fresh cup of coffee just at the right time;

Kathie Scriven, Dr. Mark A. Johnson, Debby Reilly and Becky Kellner, for editorial help and encouragement;

Pastor Jim Schuppe and Laura Strobel for wise critique and conceptual advice;

Bob Lawton, Claudia McAllister, and many other saints at Belcroft Bible Church, for their fervent prayers for God's help and guidance;

And last, but not least, my son Steven, for giving me time to work on this book by doing countless chores around the house that I should have been doing.

* * *

Author's Preface

Jesus' example of on-the-job-training inspired the concept for this book. Jesus told His disciples to follow Him and He would make them fishers of men—and so I invite you to walk through these stories with me and see how the Lord still works today—when we go fishing with Him at our side. It is my prayer that as you project yourself into these experiences, you will be greatly encouraged to be the witness and the ambassador for Jesus that we are all called to be.

You will see how the Holy Spirit answers our prayers to make divine appointments for us. And you will see how He brings scripture to mind, and how He puts words in our mouths that glorify Him…when we go forth in His power.

Just as Jesus prophesied, wickedness is increasing rapidly in these last days. More than ever, people are walking in darkness, and until they are born again, their human spirit is like an empty vacuum that must be filled! Satan and his unholy gang of murderers is always ready to fill the void.

The entertainment industry lights up the sky with the devil's tricks, while timid Christians hide their lamps under a bushel—and what's even worse—many mainline churches blatantly trash the clear teachings of the Holy Bible. Is it any wonder that church attendance is shrinking—while member-ship in cults and false religions is swelling—and millions of precious souls are being dumped into hell every day?

Brothers and sisters, let us believe God's promise of blessing in Daniel 12:3—and let us turn many to righteousness!

"And many of those who sleep in the dust of the earth shall awake, some to everlasting life, and some to shame and everlasting contempt. And they that be wise shall shine like the brightness of the firmament; and they that turn many to righteousness, as the stars forever and ever."

Introduction

A Personal Note

This book helps to fulfill a promise that I made to God during World War II. I was on board the USS Honolulu, when a Japanese torpedo hit our ship broadside in 1944, killing about 150 of my fellow crewmembers. Amazingly, our ship kept afloat and I was not hurt! But, later that night, when an airplane flew over the bow, riveting the deck all around me with machine-gun bullets, I thought surely the end had come for me!

I cried out, "Oh God, please let me live, and I promise: some day I will tell the world the *truth about war.*"

That was a strange promise for a 21-year old sailor-musician to make, because at the time, I didn't have a clue about the *truth* of anything—much less the *truth about war.*

It would take eight more years of my foolish pursuits and broken dreams before I learned the real meaning of *truth.* During an emotional crisis at age 29, I cried out again, "Oh God, if you are real, I want you to take control of my life."

Hallelujah! God answered that prayer by giving me the greatest miracle of all: I was born again according to John 3:3. Now I can keep the promise. Now I know Truth—His name is Jesus. And I know the *truth about war* as well. War is just one of many devices Satan uses to destroy people, but as Jesus said, *"Fear not them which kill the body, but are not able to kill the soul: but rather fear him which is able to destroy both soul and body in hell."* (Matthew 10:28) Only God, the author and finisher of life, has power over the soul.

And He has commissioned every born-again Christian to be His ambassador to carry His TRUTH to a lost and dying world. (2 Corinthians 5:20) I pray this book will help to motivate, teach, and encourage you to do just that.

"And the things that thou hast heard of me among many witnesses, the same commit thou to faithful men, who shall be able to teach others also."

How This Book Came About

Several years ago, God impressed upon me to keep a journal of my experiences in witnessing, which I recorded as accurately as my memory allowed. The particular experiences reported in this book were selected to represent a broad spectrum of people, situations, and approaches. They are drawn from fifty years' experience of witnessing in my corner of the world, which is mainly in Washington, DC and the surrounding Maryland suburbs.

Jesus said to His disciples, *"Follow me. I will make you fishers of men."* (Matthew 4:19) So they walked with Him down those dusty roads from town to town for the next three years. They saw how He met people's needs; and they picked up on His theology all along the way. He often taught them and others by using parables—stories that paint vivid pictures in the mind that are easily remembered. Therefore,

The purpose of this book is to show examples of how God can work through you, to influence someone's life in a major way when you go in the power of the Holy Spirit, and simply make yourself available, according to Romans 12:1: *"...present your bodies a living sacrifice, holy, acceptable unto God, which is your reasonable service."*

God uses all kinds of people to build His Kingdom. When we are born again, He empowers us to be witnesses by the same Holy Spirit that set the church of Jerusalem on fire as described in Acts, chapter 2. The Lord instructed His disciples, *"...tarry in Jerusalem until you receive power from on high."* (Luke 24:49) When the Spirit came, the whole congregation went out into a public place—praising and proclaiming *"...the wonderful works of God."* (Acts 2:11)

Witnesses simply tell the facts. They tell what they have seen and heard, and what the Lord has done for them. It's that simple! Every Christian has a unique story to tell— about how they came to trust Jesus as Lord, and how their life was changed. Your story is especially meaningful to people who knew how you lived before, and now they can see the difference Christ has made in your life. (Examples of testimonies are offered in Part Two, chapter 18.)

When Jesus healed the demoniac, Jesus did not say, "Go to Jerusalem and take a four-year course in theology, and when you have your Doctor of Divinity degree, then go tell your neighbors what I did for you." No! Neither do you need a college degree to tell people what Jesus did for you—and to explain God's simple plan of salvation.

We see many examples in the Bible of ordinary people who were touched by the Lord: the woman at the well; the blind man in John 9; Zacchaeus in Luke 19; and many others whom God used in a mighty way to witness for Him.

Brief Encounters

Shortly after I was born again, I recalled many people that God had used during my unsaved years to witness to me before I finally saw the light. Some of these people include: my dear Aunt Lottie who taught me to pray, "Now I lay me down to sleep..." when I was just a little tyke; my precious cousins Millie and Mary who took me to Sunday School; the Navy Chaplain and his Bible students who heroically carried up the scorched bodies of dead sailors from the torpedoed decks of the USS Honolulu; a girl who sang like an angel at a church I had visited in Ocean City, Maryland; my boss's wife who asked me if I knew the 23rd Psalm. The list goes on and on. Some-times, it was only a word or two; an act of kindness by a professing Christian; a scripture verse in the mail; or some-one simply saying, "I will pray for you."

Once I was having lunch at a drugstore counter, and a young lady sitting next to me abruptly turned to me and said,

"Pardon me, sir. What do you think about Jesus Christ?" I don't recall my reply, but since I was a hardheaded agnostic in those days, I doubt if my response encouraged any further conversation.

She said nothing more. However, her boldness to speak to a stranger and her simple question, combined with her earnest manner, packed a powerful punch that really made me stop and think. Although it has been many years ago, I still clearly recall her penetrating gaze that seemed to plead with me: "Sir, please understand—I just asked you the most important question in the world."

Do you see the point? God uses people—all kinds of people—to work in His garden, to bear fruit for His kingdom. As Paul wrote: "*I have planted, Apollos watered, but God gave the increase.*" (1 Corinthians 3:6) I am positive that God desires to use you somewhere in that process.

It is impossible to fail! Witnessing is a win-win thing! It is vitally important for us to realize—we are not called to save souls. Only the Holy Spirit can do that. However, we can surely plant precious seed; and we can surely sprinkle those tender shoots with the pure water of His Word. Only people can do that. And that is an indispensable part of the *greater works* that Jesus said we would do in John 14:12.

There is no greater joy than to see a wasted life being transformed by the glorious gospel of Christ! And if God used your witness as <u>part of His life-changing process</u>—that is joy unspeakable! In John 15, Jesus talked about our need to abide in the vine, bear fruit, and give glory to God. Then in verse 11, He said, "*These things have I spoken unto you that my joy might remain in you, and that <u>your joy might be full.</u>*" Hallelujah! What more can we ask? Not to mention, as we do this, we will be *building up treasures in Heaven.*

*   *   *

SEVERAL BOXED ITEMS, SIMILAR TO THE
FOLLOWING ONE, ARE SCATTERED THROUGHOUT
THIS BOOK. THEY DO NOT NECESSARILY RELATE
TO THE PRECEEDING STORY.

These may give you ideas for conversation starters; for
planting seeds; or for brief encounters when there is only
time to pass out a tract.

Use your imagination to think of interesting ways you
may communicate the gospel to a person by relating it to
their hobby, occupation, or profession. See Appendix 7.

*   *   *

What do you say to a DECORATOR?

Decorating is a fine profession. I appreciate the way you
help to make the world a more pleasant place to live. By the
way, my Father is the most creative decorator alive. Did you
see the sunset yesterday? He paints a new one in the sky
nearly every night just to give us a foretaste of how beautiful
heaven is going to be for those who believe in His Son Jesus.
How about you? Have you asked the Lord Jesus for your
free ticket to heaven? He is only a prayer away. This paper
(*hand him a tract*) will give you the details.

Part One: The Adventures

CHAPTER 1

In the Big City

You shall receive power when the Holy Ghost is come upon you; and you shall be witnesses unto me...

ACTS 1:8

My First Fishing Trip

God set this up nearly fifty years ago, but I recall it as vividly as if it just happened yesterday.

I was a layout artist with an advertising firm in Bethesda. It was a cool evening in October, 1956, and ordinarily I would be on my way home by then, however our messenger took off from work early that day, so I was stuck with his job: I had to go to the Trailways Bus Terminal in downtown Washington, DC to meet a bus coming from Baltimore; get a package of advertising proofs, show the proofs to our client, then phone our printing company to give them the corrections and an okay to run the ad.

The bus terminal was located at 12th and New York Avenue. (In those days, that was a shabby section of the city.) I arrived there just as it was beginning to get dark, and learned that the bus was not due for another 15 minutes. The waiting room was small, hot and dingy—nothing but a couple wooden benches and a pin-ball machine. No snack bar. No magazine rack. Not a place you would want to hang out. Impatient to get the job done and go home to my sweet wife, the 15 minutes wait would seem like a long time.

1

Being still just a babe in Christ, I thought about just killing time by reverting to an old habit of playing the pinball machine. But as I start to drop a coin in the slot, the Lord stopped me. I don't think He liked my idea of *killing time*...and I felt a strong urge to silently pray, "Lord, please let me spend this time in some way that will bring glory to you."

When I open my eyes, I see a big guy walk in the door and walk straight toward me. Other than needing a shave and looking like he had spent a couple nights trying to sleep on a park bench, he was fairly decent looking. I guess he was in his mid-thirties and about 6'2". (Next to my 5'10", he seemed very big). Sort of apologetically, he asked, "Could you give me a dollar to buy a glass of beer?" (There was a beer joint right across the street.)

The next few minutes really seemed weird. I had only been a believer about a year at this time, and this was my first time to experience the power of the Holy Spirit to be a witness. It seemed kind of like I was a third person, standing off to one side... just watching this little drama unfold:

Without hesitating, I looked up at him and said, "No sir. I can't give you money for you to destroy yourself. You should be ashamed! A big good-looking guy like you—bumming money to buy beer! God only gave you one brain. And you want to destroy it?"

He looked very sheepish. "I've never done this before." he said, with his voice on the verge of breaking, "I've been out of work for two weeks, and I'm dead broke."

I asked, "What kind of work do you do?"

Straightening up with a little show of confidence, he said, "I am a tile setter." Then he took out his wallet and showed me pictures of his wife and a couple of kids. He obviously was proud of his family.

I sensed he was telling the truth, so I explained to him about my job with the newspaper, and offered to place an ad (without charge) in the classified section of our paper to help him find employment.

"When I get the proofs, you can ride up with me to

Super Music City, and after I take care of business, if you're hungry, I'll buy you a hamburger or something to eat. Later, we could buy some milk and groceries for your family."

He gratefully agreed, so while waiting for the bus, we wrote an ad for JOBS WANTED. Tile setter. Hard worker. Dependable. Excellent craftsmanship. Bob Harris. Phone...

The bus arrived in a few minutes. I got the package from the driver, and we drove up to the music store on 7th St. in my brand new '56 Chevy sedan. It was rush hour and there was not a parking space in sight. So I double-parked, left the keys in the switch, and asked Bob to wait for me while I went in the store to show the proofs. I told him if a policeman made him move the car, just drive around the block until I came out.

As you might imagine, when I came back to the car about twenty minutes later, Bob was quite subdued. "I changed my mind about going for a hamburger," he said meekly. "My wife is probably worried about me. I wonder if you would just take me home. I only live a few blocks from here."

Bumper to bumper traffic on the way to his house provided plenty of time to talk. I got him talking about himself and I was surprised to learn that he had once played a guitar with some local jazz groups. We enjoyed talking about our favorite jazz musicians. I got excited when he mentioned some old 78-rpm records he had that were probably no longer available, and he insisted on loaning me a few. He was glad to have an opportunity to do me a favor.

By the time we reached his house, he sounded like he was ten years younger and had lost about forty pounds. Except for a light in a back room somewhere, the house was dark. His wife bellowed out something unintelligible with a screechy tone of voice that was not friendly...so I waited on the porch while Bob found the records. Soon, Bob emerged with a stack of old 78's. I thanked him profusely and only stayed a few minutes. Just before leaving, I said something like, "Remember, God cares about you, Bob... and believe me—prayer can change everything."

And now—the incredible rest of the story:

About two weeks later, I went back to return the records. Bob answered the door. What a transformation! He was clean-shaven, had a clean shirt on, and was all smiles since he had obtained some work through the ad. He ushered me into his brightly lit up home where his wife greeted me as a gracious hostess. And then something happened I will probably never forget:

His three little children were so excited. They crowded around me like I was a long lost uncle or something. They told me about going to Sunday School for the first time. And they insisted on giving me a beautiful picture that their Sunday School teacher had given to them—a marvelous reproduction of an oil painting of Jesus walking on the water! I really didn't want to take the picture from the little children, but they kept insisting. I guess the Lord wanted me to have it for a permanent reminder of that wonderful experience.

HALLELUJAH! What a mighty God we serve!

*   *   *

What do you say to the TRASH MAN?

My best friend is a trash collector. When I was 29 years old, my whole life was trash. I thank the Lord Jesus for picking me up out of a dump. He cleaned me up. He forgave my sins. And He gave me a holy desire to live a life that was pleasing to God. May I tell you about Him?

I am crucified with Christ. Nevertheless I live,
Yet not I, but Christ lives in me...

Teens Drinking Booze in Paper Cups

When I drove by a shopping center in Beltsville on my way home from work one evening, I saw four or five teens sitting on a curb, drinking something from paper cups. Since they were right next to a drive-in window of a liquor store, it saddened me to realize they were probably drinking alcohol. "Oh well," I thought, "it's none of my business," so I continued driving home.

After dinner, I sat on the sofa to read my Bible, but I could not concentrate. I kept reading and re-reading the same paragraph, having no comprehension of what I was reading. I couldn't get the sight of those teens out of my mind. And, it was as if the Lord said to me, "You know this stuff. You need to go tell them what it says!"

Immediately the devil zapped me with all kinds of negative and fearful thoughts of what might happen if I went there, like: "They won't listen to you. The schools have taught them evolution. They will think you are stupid. You will make a fool of yourself. A couple of those dudes looked tough. They will not like the idea of you breaking up their party with those innocent little chicks! And they might even try to break your nose for butting in."

I almost agreed with the father of lies (John 8:44), but my heavenly Father easily won the debate, pushed me off the couch and out the door. Nevertheless, I confess, I was afraid.

The shopping center was only a mile away. Since it was a warm summer evening, and more than two hours of daylight left, I decided to walk and pray along the way. After sitting all day behind a drawing board, I needed the exercise anyway, and I sure needed the time to pray.

I asked God for the power of the Holy Spirit. He reminded me of Galatians 2:20, *"I am crucified with Christ,*

5

nevertheless I live; yet not I, but Christ lives in me..." I thought I understood what the verse was saying—yet, deep within, I realized there was no reality of that in my life—it was merely words!

So, all the way there, I kept talking to the Lord and meditating on that verse. I said to myself, "If I am crucified with Christ, then I am dead. If I am dead, no one can hurt me! How can you hurt a dead person? Nevertheless, I am alive, and Christ, the champion of all preachers, the supreme evangelist, the perfect communicator Himself is living in me. He can put the words in my mouth!"

By the time I reached the battleground, all my fears were gone, and the Lord was in command. Two guys and two girls were still there. I guess they were about 14 to 18 years old. A boom box sitting on a wall was blasting some music that makes no sense to anyone over thirty, and it was so loud that a train could have roared by without attracting any attention. The kids all looked depressed—I guess the effect of alcohol was wearing off.

Walking into the midst of them, I shouted, "I know who invented music." That got their attention.

Someone answered, "You do? Who?"

"Yes! He is a good friend of mine. If you would turn that radio down, I'll be glad to tell you all about Him. In fact, I would like to introduce Him to you."

One of the girls (I'll call her Karen) turned the radio off immediately. "What do you mean—he invented music?"

"Well, first He invented birds, and He taught them how to sing. Later, when He created people—and taught them about love—the birds taught the people how to sing. Now God sent me here tonight to tell you that God created you, and He loves you far more..."

As soon as I mentioned God, one of the boys walked off, but Karen continued to listen as I talked about God's love. When I paused for a moment, Karen, nearly crying, told me why they were so sad—Her boy friend's father had died suddenly on the day before.

Wow! Now I understood why God sent me to minister to them at that exact time: their hearts were more than ready to hear the Gospel. (Chapter 21 tells several ways to share the Gospel in detail.) I don't recall all the words, but the Holy Spirit led the prayer as they confessed their sins and asked God to be their Lord and Savior. When I left them, they sat down on the curb and started reading the tracts I gave them.

The walk back home was the shortest mile I ever walked.

*   *   *

Upon reviewing this story, I am reminded there are many types of fear that hinder Christians from witnessing. I will share some more thoughts on how to overcome these fears in Appendix 8, on Page 168.

For He shall be great in the sight of the Lord, and shall drink neither wine nor strong drink; and He shall be filled with the Holy Ghost, even from His mother's womb.

An Uproar at a Liquor Store

One Saturday afternoon I went to pick up my wife from the beauty parlor, which was right next to the liquor store. Her beautician said she would not be ready for another half hour. Having a pocket testament with me, I was glad of the chance just to sit under a shade tree and read until she came out. But the Lord had another idea.

The sight of so many people streaming in and out of the liquor store—trading good money for the devil's poison— got to me! The Holy Spirit nudged me to do something—but what? I know that Jesus didn't come to condemn the world. But He came to give life and life more abundantly. "Oh Lord," I prayed, "What shall I do?"

It almost seemed as if God pointed to an ugly window sign that shouted with red paint, *A GREAT BUY,* indicating a certain bottle of liquor on display. It reminded me of a scripture I had just been reading. Opening the front door of the liquor store just a crack, I called out, "Can I see the manager please?"

Someone beckoned to me to come inside, and asked, "What do you want to talk to him about?"

I thought about 1 Thessalonians 5:22 which says *"Abstain from all appearance of evil."* So not wanting to be seen going in or out of a liquor store, I stayed on the sidewalk and called out again, "There's a problem with one of your window signs. If you will come out here, I'll show you."

The manager turned to a little man and said, "Go out and see what the big problem is." I was thankful he was just a little man because the manager was a big bruiser.

The little man was courteous and respectful as he came outside, so as kindly as possible, I spoke to him earnestly, as I pointed to the sign, "Here is the sign that is causing the problem. To say that bottle of liquor is a great buy is a misleading statement, because actually, nothing in your entire store could be called great! Everything in your store, in the long run, will only produce stupid behavior, evil thoughts, broken promises, wrecked marriages, depression, insanity, and death. Sorry to be so negative, but let me show you something that is truly great."

Quickly opening my New Testament to Luke 1:15, I pointed to the verse and read aloud to him, "*For he shall be great in the sight of the Lord, and shall drink neither wine nor strong drink: and he shall be filled with the Holy Ghost, even from his mother's womb.*" I explained, "This referred to John the Baptist, and this was a proper usage of the word great."

Before I could engage him in conversation, my wife came out of the beauty parlor and joined us on the sidewalk, so the little man took advantage of the interruption. "Thanks for sharing that," he said meekly, and slouched back into the poison shop.

I've been to that shopping mall many times since, and interestingly, I never saw the word *GREAT* appear on the window again! Praise the Lord! I never saw the little man again either. I pray he escaped from that unholy dispenser of corruption, and may he someday meet the Holy One of Israel. Then he will enjoy drinking living water from the well that never runs dry.

*   *   *

But my God shall supply all your need
according to His riches in glory by Christ Jesus.

The Unemployment Agency

Oh what a perfect place to witness! A bold brother named Alphonso Green went with me one Monday morning for the sole purpose of witnessing. When we arrived there at 9:00 am, the room was packed with unemployed people. All ages, sizes, and colors. They stand in long lines for ten or fifteen minutes; answer a few questions; and then sit in the waiting room to wait for their name to be called. That could take an hour or more, and most of them don't have a thing to read. If they have been out of work for a long time, they're ready to hear some good news.

Being aware that our ministry here is not exactly politically correct, we try to keep a low profile, as we casually walk around the room and offer people something to read. In this setting, I like to give out little booklets of "Unshackled" stories. (See chapter 17) They don't look like tracts—but they make the Gospel very clear. Then I stand back and watch.

When I see someone reading the story, and there is an empty seat next to him, I quietly sit next to him and wait for him to finish the story. Then I try to strike up a conversation by saying something like, "Well, what do you think?" or "Have you ever received the Lord Jesus as your Savior, like the man in that story?"

Where I go from there depends upon the response. I just speak the truth in love, and as always—depend upon the Holy Spirit to give me the right words to say to reach the person's heart. Before leaving, I show them the prayer for salvation on the last page of the booklet, and leave the results to God.

*   *   *

In the last day, that great day of the feast, Jesus stood and cried out , saying, If any man thirst, let him come unto me and drink. He that believeth on me, as the scripture hath said, out of his heart shall flow rivers of living water.

JOHN 7:37-38

This Encounter Cost Me a Dollar

One Sunday afternoon, Helen and I and another couple were walking along Independence Avenue in Washington, DC, when I saw a young man standing on the corner trying to sell a bottle of whiskey to people as they walked by. I felt God was leading me to witness to him—but we were on the way to a concert and our friends were anxious to get there early to get a seat up front—so 'what should I do?' I thought.

Well, God's timing was perfect. At that moment the traffic light changed, so we had to wait for it to change again before we could cross the street, so I spoke to the young man, "I'll give you a dollar for it."

He nodded agreeably, so while I fumbled for the money, I had his attention long enough to preach a short sermon: "Jesus said, *'Come unto me and drink and you shall never thirst again.'* He was talking about receiving Him as Lord and Savior... and drinking of the Holy Spirit."

When I finally produced the dollar and he handed me the bottle, I said, "I would like to tell you why I bought this. I don't want someone else to get it. Just one bottle of this poison could put someone on the wrong track that would eventually destroy his or her life. And the Bible says, *"God... is not willing that anyone should perish..."*

As he watched dumbfounded, I poured the booze in the gutter. The light changed so I handed him a tract and we hurried off to the concert. Somehow, the music was more beautiful than I had anticipated.

*   *   *

What do you say when someone asks you for direction?

We live on a street that is one of the main entrances to our city, so many times when I'm out walking or in my yard, someone will stop their car and ask me for directions. I carefully give them directions, then as I hand them a gospel tract, I say, "Incidentally, if you need direction for getting on the road that leads to heaven, I recommend that you read this. I know it is true. May God bless you.

CHAPTER 2

In the Marketplace

But thou art holy,
O thou who inhabits the praises of Israel.

PSALM 22:3

This One Bore Visible Fruit

While standing in line at the checkout counter at a local grocery store, I noticed the cashier was very friendly, and seemed to be a kindred spirit. When my turn came to be checked out, he cheerily asked, "How are you today?"

Since it was the day before Thanksgiving Day, it did not seem inappropriate to reply, "I'm thankful that I have been redeemed by the Lord Jesus Christ, and He has assigned angels to watch over me all day long."

His face lit up like a full moon, and for the next three or four minutes as he checked out my stuff, we had an old-fashioned revival meeting right there in the Giant Food Store, with "Amen" and "Praise the Lord" reverberating all over the place. What joy to meet such a turned-on brother!

As I shopped there regularly, within a few weeks, we became pretty well-acquainted. One evening when he saw me coming, he took a break and joined me outside on the sidewalk for some serious fellowship. After I became satisfied that he was standing on solid Bible doctrine, I told him about my involvement in a weekly ministry at Crownsville Mental Hospital, and invited him to come with myself and others from my church. He came. He preached. He was a real blessing to the patients.

He arranged with the hospital volunteer services to go with others from his church to a juvenile ward on Saturday mornings.

See how the Lord expands His work.

13

Jesus said unto him, "I am the way, the truth, and the
life. No one comes to the Father but by me."

JOHN 14:6

Trading Dunkin Donuts for Living Bread

I was the only customer that afternoon in Dunkin Donuts in Beltsville, so I had a good opportunity to say a few words to the clerk and give him one of my favorite gospel tracts: on the front is that famous photo of the earth taken from outer space. The headline reads: "What Single Event in Human History Had the POWER to SPLIT TIME?"

It opens to a gatefold with bold graphics: B.C. on the left side, and A.D. on the right. They are divided by a symbol of the cross and the caption reads: "When the fullness of time was come, God sent forth His Son." Then it opens to a large "CELEBRATE JESUS" spread across the four panels. The gospel message is presented very clearly. (It's available from Celebrate Jesus 2000, 4200 North Point Parkway, Alpharetta, Georgia 30022) As I was about to get in my car and drive off, I saw the clerk come outside, sit on the curb, and begin to read the tract. He looked friendly, so I went over and sat down beside him. He nodded to me and kept reading. When he finished reading, I simply said to him, "Well my friend, what do you think?"

He smiled and said, "I'm a Muslim."

I spontaneously replied in a somewhat joking manner, "You don't have to stay that way."

He seemed amused at my brashness, and he seemed open for conversation. So after trading names and a few pleasantries, I said, "I don't know much about your religion, Neal, but I have heard that you believe that Jesus was a prophet. Is that right?"

"Yes." he replied, "That is correct."

"Well then, I have a question for you. Does a prophet always tell the truth?"

"Sure, a prophet tells the truth."

"I agree. In the Old Testament, if a man that spoke like a prophet foretold something that did not come to pass, he was stoned to death. Yes, Jesus was a prophet. But He was much more than that."

Neal listened with interest so I continued, "Neal, do you know what Jesus said about himself?"

"No."

"Jesus said, *If you've seen me, you have seen the Father. I and the Father are one.* That's in the New Testament." I took out my Gideon pocket Testament and showed him a few more verses. "Have you read the New Testament, Neal?"

"No."

A customer drove in the lot, so I had to hurry because I knew Neal would have to go in and wait on the customer. I grabbed a paperback Bible out of my car, stuck it in his hands, and said, "I suggest that you begin reading at the Gospel of John—and you will see what the prophet Jesus said about Himself." I turned down a corner of the page to mark the spot. "I'll see you later."

A few days later, I dropped by to see him. Neal recognized me with a big grin—and he wouldn't let me pay for my donut and coffee. The store was full of customers, so I sat down to wait for a chance to talk with him. When the last customer left, Neal came over to my table. At this point, I decided to try to build a deeper relationship with him—to show him that I really cared about him. So I inquired about his family, career interests, etc. We got along great. I invited him to come to my house some time to shoot pool. He said he would enjoy that very much. But then customers interrupted our visit, so I took off.

About a week later when I went to Dunkin Donuts, we only had time for a brief conversation. Neal was happy that he had been promoted as a manager. When I asked him if he had been reading the Bible, he said, "Yeah, but my father saw me reading it and really gave me hell! He said, 'Don't you let me catch you reading that again.'

So I said, "I'm sorry to hear that. But you know how it is with old folks. They get set in their ways. It's hard to reason with them."

Sometimes the Holy Spirit tells me to keep quiet, and this was one of those times. I felt that Neal had a deep respect for his father, so I needed to tread lightly. In parting, I just said that I would pray for God to reveal His truth to him and his dad.

The next time I went to Dunkin Donuts, one of the employees told me that Neal had been transferred to another store—but nobody knew where. So, I'm sorry to say, I lost touch with him. But I thank God—He used me to plant some seed! God knows exactly where Neal is ... and I'm praying He will send others along to water that seed.

*   *   *

For we know that all things work together for good
for those who love the Lord,
and are the called according to His purpose.

ROMANS 8:28

Praise God for Computer Jams

On this particular morning, I thought this would simply be a routine visit to my bank office. It turned out to be another one of God's divine appointments.

After a short wait, I was ushered into a consultant's private office. She was a smart looking, middle-aged woman named Emily. She looked as though she could use some cheering up. After I stated my business to her, she mechanically began filling out forms on her computer. However, when the computer did not cooperate, she became a little irritated and apologized for the delay, so I said with a smile, "Not to worry. It's no problem. We can just claim Romans 8:28."

That went right past her. No reaction. She just kept murmuring something about cheap computers. So I tried again, "Do you know Romans 8:28?"

Emily smiled politely, but ignored the question. She finally got the computer to act properly and resumed chattering about money matters. Ordinarily in this type of situation, I would simply give up talking about anything spiritual and go on with business as usual, but the Holy Spirit had a different idea: I leaned toward her and spoke more forcefully, "I asked you a question." Now I had her attention.

She came out of her office manners mode, "What?"

"I asked if you knew Romans 8:28."

"No. What's that mean?"

"It's what I call God's golden promise. It's in the Bible, in the Book of Romans, chapter 8, verse 28. It says that all things work together for good for those who love the Lord and are called according to His purpose. Isn't that a wonderful promise? You see, when the computer didn't behave and caused a delay, I just accepted the fact that God used that for His purpose. I may never understand the details, but we can imagine… For example, perhaps if I had left here five minutes sooner I would have been involved in a serious automobile accident. Only God knows what…"

Interrupting, Emily got excited, "Funny you mentioned that!" she said, "Just yesterday, I had a very narrow escape in my car. I could have been killed, if I had been there two seconds before!"

"Wow! Thank God, He spared your life! That shows He has an important purpose for your life—just like the Bible says. And maybe God caused this computer glitch today, just to give us an opportunity to talk together." Her eyes were agreeing with me. And I felt the Lord telling me to say, "Emily, I would like to pray for you." She took my hands while we prayed and I asked the Lord to show her the special purpose He had for her life.

She thanked me for the prayer, and then I asked her, "Emily, do you have a church that you enjoy?"

"No. I do believe in God, but I haven't been to church in years. I don't know of a good church near where I live."

We talked a few more minutes. I asked where she lived

so I could recommend a good church. Later, I inquired from a friend who knew her area and three days later I was able to phone her and recommend a good church near her home. She promised to visit it the following Sunday.

Two weeks later, I went to the bank again and stuck my head in her office just to say "Hi." She was talking to a customer seated across the desk from her, and suddenly in the middle of a sentence, she saw me standing at the door. Her face broke into a beautiful smile and she jumped out of her chair, ran over to me, and gave me a big hug! Customers were waiting to see her, so we only had time for a few words, but she said, "I'm going to that church tomorrow and my sister is going with me."

Now you know how God can use a computer jam.

*   *   *

What do you say to an ATHLETE?

My best friend was the strongest man that ever lived. He was murdered in Jerusalem and buried. But three days later He came back to life. Do you know who I'm talking about?

Look unto me, and be ye saved, all the ends of the earth; for I am God, and there is none else.

ISAIAH 45:22

I Beg Your Pardon, Mr. Buddha

A very obese statue of Buddha was laughing at me as I waited my turn at the cashier's counter of a Chinese restaurant. I had just enjoyed a delicious lunch and I simply wanted to pay my bill and be on my merry way. But God set up an appointment that could not be denied: the pretty little Chinese cashier saw the book in my hand and asked me, "Is that a good book?"

I was in a big hurry, but God goes by a different clock. So I said, "Yes! It is absolutely the best book ever written. It's the New Testament." Suddenly I forgot why I was in such a hurry. "Have you ever read it?"

She had a sweet smile when she simply answered, "I am a Buddhist."

Thankfully, other customers came to pay their bill, which gave me time to think and pray about what I would say next.

I felt led to ask, "I wonder, did you grow up in a family that is Buddhist? (This has become a stock question that I often ask people of other faiths.)

"Yes. All my family is Buddhist."

"I know how that is. My dad was an agnostic, so for many years I accepted his beliefs. But when I got in the Navy and old enough to think for myself, I met some smart people who influenced me to investigate other religions. But

I don't know much about Buddhism. Isn't it more of a philosophy than a religion?"

She started to answer, but another customer interrupted, giving me time to think of a better question: "Do you believe that when you die, you will go to heaven?"

"We believe in reincarnation," she said, ever so sweetly.

"Oh... that's kind of sad..." I acted shocked. "You think you could come back to life as a dog or a cat or a...?" I had started to say a flea or a tick, but—thank God, she interrupted—because that may have sounded offensive.

She said, "Well that wouldn't be so bad. I have a pet dog, and he has a pretty good life."

Oh boy, thank God for more customer interruptions, giving me time to pray for more wisdom of where to go next. "By the way, my name is Warren. What's your name?"

"Susan."

"Susan, May I ask you a personal question?"

She just smiled, so I took that as a yes. "Is your mother still living?"

"Yes. She is still living."

"Good. That's a blessing. But you know Susan... some day your mother will die. Now, wouldn't it be great to know for sure that when you die, you will see your mother again? And she will have a brand new heavenly body that will never die?"

Now she looked interested, so I continued, "Susan, God loves you more than you can even imagine. If you read this book (it was the Promise Keeper's version with the plan of salvation in the front) it will tell you all about our wonderful Jesus—and you will learn how you can receive the gift of eternal life."

"You say eternal life is a _gift_?"

"Yes, a free gift, for everyone that has faith in the Lord Jesus. He bought us a ticket to heaven when He died on the cross to pay the penalty for our sins."

Just then, another customer came by to pay his check, and overheard some of our conversation. He had God's wisdom and the joy of Jesus written all over his face. As he was leaving, he said, "That's right! Jesus paid it all!"

"Susan, if you would like to read this, I'll be glad to give it to you. Let me encourage you to start with the Gospel of John. Here, I'll turn down the page for you."

"Does it tell about heaven?" Susan asked.

"Yes...The last chapter of Revelation says heaven is a place where there will be no sickness, no death, no sorrow, no tears, and I guess, best of all—no sin. And 1st Corinthians 2:9 says, "...*Eye has not seen, nor ear heard, neither has it entered into the heart of man, the things which God has prepared for them that love Him.*"

Susan asked, "When will you come back so I can return the book?"

"No need to return it. You may keep it. A Christian who owns a used bookstore gives me paperback Bibles because she knows that I give them away. But I'll see you again soon." More paying customers were coming, so I felt it was time to go.

I've been going there for lunch occasionally. Susan is always friendly, but does not indicate much interest in Jesus yet. I will keep praying for her salvation.

Thank you, Mr. Buddha. Your food is delicious—but your religion is fictitious.

*   *   *

CHAPTER 3

Strangers in the Street

*I will sing of the mercies of the Lord forever;
with my mouth will I make known
thy faithfulness to all generations*

PSALM 89:1

Singing the Gospel to Construction Workers

As I was taking my lunchtime walk with the Lord, I became excited about a song I had just finished writing, and I couldn't wait to sing it to someone. As I walked along humming the tune, I approached a construction site and saw a couple of carpenters lounging near the sidewalk eating lunch. After exchanging a few pleasantries, they seemed quite friendly, so I seized the opportunity and announced, "I'm excited about a new song I just finished writing! I would like to sing it for you? I'd like to know what you think about it."

"OK," they said, so I sang it. It's called GOD JUST SPOKE ... It's sort of a condensed version of the Bible from Genesis to Revelation, and it makes the gospel very clear.

GOD JUST SPOKE—and the world appeared.
The sun and the moon and the earth was here
The whole universe precisely put in gear
The birds and the bees and the flowers and trees
The beasts in the field and the fish in the seas
That's all. He just spoke. Amen.

GOD JUST SPOKE—let us make a man
From the dust of the earth—just a hunk of clay
He made a splendid man like you see today
He loved him so much that he gave him a wife

22

And put them in the garden with the tree of life
That's all. He just spoke. Amen

Now everything God did so far
was just by speaking the Word
But one day Satan came around
And nothing but lies were heard
Adam and Eve made a big mistake
When they believed that old snake
Their sinful ways would multiply
Until the whole world would die

It's no joke! We had lost our way
The all-mighty God had not a word to say
Not even God can speak a sin away
When God gives His Word but we disobey
We lose all our joy and there's hell to pay
Bad news! It's no joke! Oh no

Holy smoke—up on Mt. Sinai
Ten laws from God upon a rock were spelled
Moses showed the people but they soon rebelled
Now we're gonna burn in a fiery lake
A smoky place for sinners and the devil snake
Bad news! It's no joke! Oh no

People's hearts grew cold and hard as stone
God's Word didn't mean a thing
Heaven was wasted—the way was not known
His angels forgot how to sing
Nothing could be done but let Jesus, His Son
Hang on that bloody tree
He paid the fee for our sinful fun
Now we can have heaven for free

GOD JUST SPOKE—And He's calling us
To trust in His Word and believe in Him
To open up our hearts and let His Spirit in
He fills us with love and He walks by our side
And prepares us a place where we'll always abide
Good news! He just spoke.

They listened very attentively and one remarked, "Good song. I like it."

It was time to return to work, so that was the extent of the encounter. Anyhow, they heard the gospel.

*　　*　　*

24

...Christ in you, the hope of glory.

COLOSSIANS 1:27

Can You Show Me Jesus?

I wish you could have been with us that day! You would probably have to see this to understand what's so special about it. So let me try to paint the picture for you:

It's about three o-clock in the afternoon in the middle of July. Several small churches in Northeast Washington DC combined forces to stage a block party in a residential area of row houses. One of the leaders purchased a few of my Gospel signs to use for the event so when I delivered them I decided to stay and take part in the ministry.

The church folks went all out to spread the gospel to the neighbors. City Police roped off the street at both ends of the block, and the city provided a large trailer at one end of the block with a stage for the music, worship dances, and fiery preaching over the PA system. Someone also set up a stand with hot dogs and soft drinks.

A few people teamed up to go out into the neighborhood and circulate flyers inviting others to come. I teamed up with Veada Ryels-Lewis, a young woman who bubbles over with the joy of the Lord.

After a short prayer together, we walked about three blocks to H Street looking for people who need the Lord. Although H Street is usually busy with shoppers, not many were out there that day. The sun was blazing—and there was not a patch of shade anywhere. It was just too blamed hot for anyone to be out there if they could possibly find any place else to go.

However, we finally spotted one little man as he came out of some air-conditioned store. His face had a lot of history written on it, and it was all bad. Scars on top of scars. If anyone looked like they needed the Lord, he did. So we zeroed in on him.

It was much too hot to waste time with preliminaries, so

25

Veada cut right to the chase. She said: "Pardon us sir, but the Lord sent us here to tell you about Jesus. Do you know Him as your Lord and Savior?"

He said, "Jesus? Jesus? Who is this Jesus? I've heard about Socrates, Plato, and I've seen Louis Farrakhan, and Martin Luther King Jr. But who is Jesus? Can you show me a picture of Jesus?"

It was hard to tell where this man was coming from. I had the feeling that he knew something, but was just testing us. The Holy Spirit knew exactly what to say. "Yes. I can show you Jesus." I moved in closer until only about ten inches separated my nose from his, and I said, "Look into my eyes; and look into her eyes! You will see Jesus. He lives in us...so that we can tell you about God's love for you."

Before we could say more, the man threw his arms around us, gave us a big hug, a big smile... and went on his way.

I probably won't recognize him in heaven, because all his scars will be gone. And of course, everyone there will be wearing a big smile.

*   *   *

What do you say to an ENGINEER?

My Father was a wonderful engineer. He designed the entire universe, set all the stars and planets in motion... and now He holds it all together! Aren't you glad that He created you and He has a wonderful purpose for your life? He loves you more than you can imagine. Do you know Him?

---

*What shall it profit a man to gain the whole world
but lose his own soul?*

MARK 8:36

Chasing a Tree hugger on Route 1

One afternoon while driving along a busy highway in
Beltsville, Maryland, I saw a man running along the shoulder
of the road carrying a blazing torch. I was not able to read
the message on his T-shirt, but I was so impressed to see a
man expend such energy for whatever cause, I decided I had
to talk to him.

Making a U-turn, I slowed down and drove along side of
him for a short distance, and gestured that I wanted to talk to
him, but he made it clear that he would not stop running for
anything or anybody. (He reminded me of Forest Gump.) I
remarked to my wife, "The Kingdom of God sure could use
a man with that kind of determination to promote a cause."

So I drove on ahead of him for a short distance, parked the car and tried to run in step with him. "What's happening man?," I shouted.

No intelligible answer.

"What are you promoting?"

"You know—ecology, man."

"What do you mean?" (I can't run and think clearly at the same time.)

"Like trees and stuff."

"Good cause." I'm starting to breathe pretty hard by now so I figure it's time to get to the point. So I holler, "What do you think about Jesus?"

"Cool. But we gotta save the trees!"

I was too tired to pursue this conversation any further, so I gave one parting gasp: "Jesus Christ is Lord! He came to save sinners like you and me."

I'm not sure that he heard that. The smoke from his torch was stinging my eyes—and I had fallen too far behind.

He just kept on running towards Baltimore.

*　　*　　*

How Do You Respond to Someone That Tells You to "Take It Easy"?

You could say, "My rest is in Jesus. The Bible says "He is my Sabbath rest." How about you? Do you know Him?"

Just depend on God to direct the conversation from there.

And of course, you can always give them a tract.

CHAPTER 4

Witnessing on the Job

*Let your light so shine before men,
that they may see your good works and glorify
your Father, which is in heaven.*

MATTHEW 5:16

A Verse Personified

I met Tom Fox when I was working for a printing company as a graphic artist. Tom was hired to operate an offset press and a camera. Before he came on board, the basement area where he would work was a disaster—trash, dust and clutter were everywhere.

On his first day on the job, without a word of complaint, Tom just started transforming the place. Within a week, he had rejuvenated everything! What a difference—everything was organized and spic and span—the old press was cleaned, oiled, polished, and turning out beautiful work. It was hard to believe it was the same place.

Although it was a high-pressure job with a heavy workload, Tom was always cheerful. Everyone soon learned —by his walk—<u>and</u> his talk, that he was the kind of man a Christian ought to be.

When it came to verbal witnessing, Tom was no slouch at that either. He could offer a biblical perspective on just about any subject that came up. Once, one of the pressmen asked him for his opinion regarding divorce. I overheard him answer, "My opinion isn't worth two cents, but I can tell you what Jesus said about it. But not during working hours. Can we talk at lunchtime?" He practiced the old-fashioned principle of giving the boss an honest day's work for a day's pay.

We became great friends. And I'm sure everyone

noticed the friendship and joy that we shared as Christians—which answers in part the prayers of Jesus in John 17:21 *"...that they all may be one... That the world may believe that thou hast sent me."*

I am reminded of a woman in my church that testified that she always tried to get to work 30 minutes early each day. This gave her many opportunities to witness to fellow workers before her workday began—or, she could always spend that time reading her Bible! Unless we have the kind of job where we can talk without interfering with the work, we had better save our preaching until lunchtime, or before or after working hours.

On one of my jobs, I frequently used the office copier and paper to copy doctor bills for my wife's insurance. I always offered to pay for the supplies, but they wouldn't accept the money. They said it would complicate bookkeeping too much. So to make up for it, when I left the company, I donated a box of small tools for camera maintenance, which I had purchased with my own money. Little things like that—added to what we preach—can be a strong testimony.

*   *   *

But ye are a chosen generation, a royal priesthood, a holy nation, a peculiar people; that ye should show forth the praises of Him who has called you out of darkness into His marvelous light.

1 PETER 2:9

Two Weeks Before Christmas

I had been praying for an opportunity to share the gospel with fellow workers in the graphics art department of an advertising agency I worked for in the '80's. Note how God answered this prayer:

Walking through the woods at lunchtime, I saw a holly tree loaded with red berries. I broke off a small branch and prayed for wisdom to relate this to Christmas, and provide a natural way to share the gospel with my co-workers.

Returning to the office about five minutes before lunchtime was over, six of my associates were still sitting around the table in the conference room. As I entered the room singing "fa la la la la la la la la" ("Deck the Halls,") another guy joined in with the words. Someone else made cracks about a Maryland State law, which forbids the cutting of holly, so I explained that it was growing on the edge of a lot, which was being bulldozed for new construction. Then I hung the holly over a picture frame where all could see it.

Now that I had everyone's attention, I took a deep breath and said, "I used to feel very humbug about Christmas. It has become so commercial." Then looking at one co-worker in particular, I said, "You recall how it was, Mark, when we worked in retail advertising, how we got so sick of designing Christmas ads and drawing Santa Claus. But now, Hallelujah for Christmas! I've decided to enjoy it for what it really is."

Pointing to the holly, I said, "The red berries remind us of the shed blood of Jesus that washes away our sins; the evergreen reminds us of the greatest gift of all: the gift of eternal life that God gives to everyone who receives Jesus as their personal Savior and Lord of their life. No more bah-humbug for me. From now on it's: Hallelujah! Praise the Lord that we can celebrate Christmas."

Mark then said jokingly, "I believe we just got used as guinea pigs for Warren to practice his sermon for tomorrow night at the mental hospital."

"No, Mark," I replied, "My prayer is that everyone here would come to know the joy of the Lord."

Six souls came for lunch—and Jesus fed them the Living Bread, come down from heaven!

Incidentally, one of those co-workers, Art Landerman, who at that time was a hard-drinking, pot-smoking, guitar player in rock bands, phoned me about ten years later and ecstatically told me that he had been born again—and he was reading the Gideon New Testament that I had given him.

He phones me frequently to share some new thing God is doing in his life—like singing a duet in church with his new beautiful Christian wife. Not only that, since trading rock music for the Rock of Ages, Landerman has become a first-rate designer and illustrator.

*　　*　　*

> *And out of the ground made the Lord God to grow every tree that is pleasant to the sight, and good for food; The tree of life also in the midst of the garden, and the tree of knowledge of good and evil.*

GENESIS 2:9

A 30" x 24" Christmas Card

For me, it was another Christmas at another ad agency, and another opportunity to be a witness. Out of fifty-some employees, only five, including me, professed to be Christians, and we had to keep the lid on our enthusiasm for Jesus most of the time.

The people who worked in the top echelon of the agency were very worldly, ambitious, materialistic, and rich with the things of this world—and much too busy to be concerned with spiritual things. So they sent employees 'season's greeting' cards that displayed clever, amusing, sophisticated, politically correct designs that were careful to ignore the birthday of (*shhh*) Jesus. But this year I chose not to mail a card to anyone in the company. The Lord gave me another idea. This Christmas would probably be my last one here, so I decided to be bolder than usual.

The traditional office party began at noon on the day before. The secretaries had decorated a plastic tree. Some of the execs brought their wives in. Everybody dressed up, put on a happy face, stood around eating tons of good food, swilling punch, and amusing each other with funny stories, while the vice president went around handing out the annual bonus checks. The climax came when the president gave his eloquent appreciation speech, reported on the progress the company had made that year, and graciously thanked everyone for their excellent contributions. *Applause, applause.*

After all the hubbub slacked off a little, it was time to make my missionary journeys into the kitchen. (All during the year, I had opportunities to share my faith with the other artists I worked in close contact with, but I rarely had contact with people in other departments, especially the corporation executives.)

Approaching each individual one at a time, I said something like this, "Walter, I want to thank you for the beautiful card you sent me. I designed my own card this year, but it was too big to mail, so I hung it on the wall in the kitchen. Have you seen it yet? Then please come with me and let me show it to you." Then I escorted him or her into the kitchen.

The "Tree of Life" planted on either side of a pure river of water, and bearing twelve different kinds of fruit, dominated the 30" x 20" oil painting. At the base of the tree on the left side in script letters was the verse from Genesis that said,

You may freely eat from the Tree of Life.

On the right side, these words:

May your Christmas be delicious...
and your new year nutritious.

Each piece of fruit had a clear film overlay imprinted with a Gospel verse. The trunk of the tree appeared to have a carving of GOD LOVES YOU with the typical arrow-pierced heart symbol, and again, a film overlay with an imprint of John 3:16 (except the agency logo was substituted for *the world*). The painting stayed on the wall right over the coffee pot until New Year's Eve, where probably everyone saw it. It served as a lunchtime conversation piece for several persons, and I thank God—that was one illustration I really felt inspired to create that Christmas.

*　　*　　*

But my God shall supply all your needs
according to his riches in glory by Christ Jesus

PHILLIPIANS 4:19

I Found Joy at a Parking Meter

While putting coins in a parking meter one morning, I noticed a lady, her back towards me, also feeding a meter near mine. It was a beautiful spring day, so I impulsively called out, "My, hasn't the Lord given us a beautiful day!"

She turned around and practically exploded with "Praise the Lord! Hallelujah!" We were both delighted to meet another Christian!

This was one of those special blessings the Lord gives His children! It was not for planting seeds, or for watering! It was simply for the joy and encouragement the Lord provides by connecting us with another brother or sister at the precise time when we are in need of fellowship.

For me, it was my first day at a new job, which is usually somewhat stressful. As we began walking in the same direction, we naturally struck up a conversation and discovered we both worked in the same building, and we had many mutual interests. So what I intended for a simple seed planting, ripened into a fruitful friendship in the next few months.

One way it was fruitful—Joyce was also a Sunday School teacher, as well as a mother of two children—so when we frequently met for lunch in the cafeteria, she was able to give me many good ideas about teaching my Sunday School class.

One of the things she taught me was how to use drama: the children are given roles to play; they memorize their lines and act out the Bible stories. They really enjoy it—and what better way to learn God's wonderful truths?

We eventually lost touch with each other after I changed jobs, but I still thank God for every remembrance of Joyce. What a blessing!

Joyce—if you're reading this—thanks for the memory and may God bless you richly.

*   *   *

How do you respond to a person that says "Take care."

The Bible encourages us to cast all our cares upon Jesus, because He cares for us. In fact, He cares for us so much that He took the punishment that we deserved by paying for all of our sins when He hung on the cross at Calvary. And just by believing, trusting and obeying Jesus we can experience the miracle of being 'born again' according to the Gospel of John. Pease read this for details. *Hand them a gospel tract.*

CHAPTER 5

Praise God in Public Meetings

Do not worry about how or what you will speak.
but it will be given you in that hour what you will speak, for
it is not you who speak, but the Spirit of your Father who
speaks in your behalf.

MATTHEW 10:19-20

Preaching the Gospel at City Hall

A nightclub featuring topless dancers was located on Route 1, close to the University of Maryland, where, incidentally there had been several charges of rape by college students on campus. For some time the local newspaper had been running an article about an ongoing dispute between this club and a young pastor from a nearby church who was fighting to have this den of corruption shut down. He circulated petitions and spoke against it at community gatherings. However, it did not appear he was getting much support from the authorities.

Knowing that Satan uses these kinds of things to tempt many young men to indulge in the sin that destroys both body and soul, I became very burdened about it!

The newspaper announced the date of a final hearing on this issue at City Hall. One evening, while I was in prayer, the Lord impressed me to go to that hearing. I could not imagine what I could accomplish, because my knowledge of the laws that govern these things is zilch! But the Holy Spirit brought this scripture to mind: Jesus said to His disciples, *"Ye shall be brought before governors and kings for my sake, for a testimony against them... Take no thought of how or what ye shall speak: for it shall be given you in that same hour what ye shall speak. For it is not ye that speak, but the Spirit of your Father which speaketh in you."* (Matthew

10:18-19)

God also impressed upon me to dress up in my Sunday suit and tie, and get there early. I was amazed at the way the Lord set this up: when I arrived, there were two empty seats up front, right next to the former mayor. When I sat next to him, he greeted me as if we were old friends! Then a few minutes later, the new mayor of College Park arrived, greeted us cordially, and sat next to me. So there I am—a nobody—seated in the most prominent place between two mayors! I believe the councilmen were duly impressed.

I learned that the young preacher had spoken very passionately about morals in previous meetings; and he passed the word to me that it would probably be better if I did not say too much; so I promised to be brief. The hearing was not interesting—a lot of legal mumbo jumbo and no decision was made. Nearly an hour went by before I was given an opportunity to speak.

The chairman said, "If anyone else wishes to make a statement, raise your hand." So I did. The chairman asked me to come forward to the microphone and state my name and address. I still had no idea what to say, but just as the Lord promised—He put the words in my mouth:

"I only wish to say, we can be sure that some day we will all be judged by a much higher court for the decisions we make here." Then I started to walk back to my chair. But the chairman called out to me, sort of sarcastically,

"Are you saying Mr. Sears, that if we judge wrongly here, we will all go to hell?"

I answered, "No sir. God is merciful. He said, *If we confess our sins, He will be faithful and just to forgive us our sins, and cleanse us from all unrighteousness.*" (1 John 1:9). The Bible also says, "*God so loved the world that He gave His only begotten Son, so that whosoever believes in Him would not perish, but would have everlasting life.*" (John 3:16).

He said, "Thank you, Mr. Sears."

I said, "Praise the Lord." and the meeting was adjourned. Later I learned we were being televised for the local news and probably would be seen by hundreds of people.

I'm happy to say that shortly after that, the club was forced to close. Did my testimony have anything to do with it? I don't know. Nevertheless, I thank the Lord for calling me to be a witness at City Hall!

*　　*　　*

And all things are of God, who has
reconciled us to Himself by Jesus Christ,
And has given to us the ministry of reconciliation.

2 CORINTHIANS 5:18

A Pocket of Sin in Beltsville

This notice appeared in "The Beltsville News:" "CHRISTIANS WILL HOLD A SPECIAL MEETING at the Martin Luther King High School at 7:00 p.m. Friday to discuss the problem of a little pocket of sin in the old part of Beltsville. Right on Route 1, there is an adult bookstore, a house of prostitutes—disguised as a massage parlor, and a drive-in movie that features X-rated films. What can we do about it? Everyone is urged to attend this meeting."

As I prayed about it, the Lord impressed me that He wanted to use me in that meeting—and I must dress up in my gray suit and tie and get there early. I found a front seat right next to the speaker's platform.

By 7 o'clock the large assembly room was packed. The chairman introduced the speaker, a local politician, and the meeting began—surprisingly without even a word of prayer.

The speaker was long-winded as he reported on the many efforts they had made in the past to clean up the sleaze. He gave a lot reasons why they had not been successful; and he recited many legal problems that must be dealt with, such as zoning laws. But, although he lacked confidence that anything could be done, he promised that they would continue to work through legal channels to solve the problem. The chairman then opened the meeting for folks to ask questions.

Suddenly, there was a violent disturbance by the doors at the rear of the hall. Apparently, some of the devil's people tried to break in and disrupt the meeting. Some men blocked the entrance and kept them from entering the building. Nevertheless, people took this as a signal that the meeting was over and everyone began to walk toward the exit. At this point, the Holy Spirit told me why I was there:

The gray suit leaped up to the platform, grabbed the microphone, and said something like this: "Please wait a moment folks." Everyone stopped walking and turned around to listen. "Since this meeting was announced in the newspaper as a Christian meeting, let us close with prayer."

In a moment the room became silent and the Holy Spirit put the words in my mouth. As near as I can recall, it came forth something like this: "Our Father and our God, we pray to you now in the name of our Lord and Savior Jesus Christ. Please help us to love you more... and help us to hate the things that you hate. We know that people who love the Lord Jesus do not patronize prostitutes, and they do not buy pornography. We know that those who love Jesus do not have any desire for booze. Oh God, please help all your people to share the Gospel... and to glorify the wonderful name of Jesus—because He alone has the power to drive the devil out of Beltsville. Amen." And about 200 people said, "Amen!"

The last time I looked, the drive-in movie was gone; the whorehouse was gone; and the adult bookstore has been replaced by a CVS Pharmacy.

*　　*　　*

CHAPTER 6

Class Acts

Heaven and earth may pass away,
but my words will never pass away.

MATHEW 24:35

Toastmasters Critique Jesus Talk

You have probably heard people say, "I will witness when an opportunity comes along." The problem with that is, when opportunities do come, (often at unexpected times) people don't recognize them, and if they do recognize them, they may not be ready to take full advantage of them. This story is about recognizing an extra-ordinary opportunity... and getting prepared for it.

Dr. Sam Shen, a friend from my church at that time, invited me to attend a special eight-week course at the Toastmaster's Club to learn the art of public speaking. "It costs $30," he said. "You will have three opportunities to speak in front of thirty people. They will listen very carefully in order to critique your talk. And best of all—you will be able to speak on any topic you wish."

Wow! What an opportunity, I thought: "Three chances to share Jesus with thirty people for $30. Not bad! For just $1.00 per person, I will have their undivided attention on three separate occasions." I went for it!

The title of my first speech was: "What makes a great communicator?" And this was my opening paragraph:

"I have pondered that question many times, and I am thankful for the things we are learning here with Toastmasters. However, if we really wish to excel at communicating, we could all profit by studying the words and the life of the greatest communicator that ever lived. As He said, *'Heaven and earth shall pass away, but my words shall not pass away.'* (Matthew 24:35) Of course, I am talking about Jesus Christ. I encourage you to read the New Testament and ask yourself, 'How can it be that the words of Jesus have made such an impact on the world? How can it be that the words He spoke nearly 2000 years ago are still changing the course of history?" (You may see a complete copy of my talk in Appendix 2)

My next topic was "A Trip to the Holy Land," recounting my personal trip to Jerusalem the previous year. And my third topic was "The Miracle of Being Born Again" —my conversion experience.

Several people told me they enjoyed my talks. After the last class was over, one young lady walked to the parking lot with me. She said, "I wish I could have the kind of faith that you do." I told her, "Faith is also a gift from God. It comes by hearing His word." (Romans 10:17)

I gave her a Bible (I usually keep a few in the car) and a good salvation tract and encouraged her to read the Gospel of John several times—and pray for God to give her the faith to believe in Him.

Thank you, Jesus—for giving me those three remarkable opportunities to share my faith with thirty precious souls.

*   *   *

Author's Note

Although we should always depend upon the Holy Spirit when witnessing, often, sharing our faith falls into the same category that so much else does—practice, practice, practice—will make us more effective, give us confidence, and help us to feel comfortable in most situations.

*   *   *

For God is the King of all the earth:
sing ye praises with understanding.

PSALM 47:7

A Song-Writing Class Gets Blessed

What a wonderful opportunity! Senior citizens can take classes at a community college in Prince George's County, Maryland, for free. No tuition required! Therefore, after retiring from my full-time career, I took several classes in songwriting. Not only was I able to improve my skills, but it also gave me many chances to witness, as students were required to sing their songs to the class for criticism.

One student cracked me up when I sang my song, "A Beautiful Born Again Town." He said, "I think this would be a great song if he took out all that stuff about Jesus."

At any rate, I was obedient to God's Word in Psalm 98:1, which says; *"O sing unto the Lord a new song; for He hath done marvelous things."* So, about twenty young college students and the instructor heard about a town where "the love of Jesus never leaves us... and His Words are making all things new."

My best song came from a class assignment that was to write a lyric telling a story structured on a progression of time. So I wrote, "A Fisherman called Peter" which ends with, "When Peter saw the risen Christ, he'd never doubt again. The fisherman called Peter now would fish for men."

*   *   *

How then, shall they call on Him in whom they have not
believed? And how shall they believe in Him
of whom they have not heard?
And how shall they hear without a preacher?

ROMANS 10:14

Three Muslims Came to Our Bible Study

Just when I think I've written the last story in this chapter,
God does something else which is too special to omit.

Rev. Bob Lawton, a missionary to medical students, got
me involved in leading Bible studies twice a week at Prince
George's Community College. Then God provided three
other Bible teachers—John Thrift, Charles Reeves, and
David Heiss to assist.

We have a table in the Student Center for giving out
literature and inviting students to the Bible Study. On this
day, a few Christians came by and picked up copies of *The
Daily Bread.* But after two hours, only one person,
Stephanie, a Christian who had attended last year, said she
would come to the Bible Study. We packed up the stuff and
headed upstairs to the conference room.

A student got on the elevator with me and I invited him
to attend the study. He told me he was a Muslim. As we
walked down the hall together, I gave my stock response that
I always ask Muslims. "You believe Jesus was a prophet,
right?"

"Yes, we believe He was a prophet," he answered.

By this time, we had reached our office, which was
located across the hall from the Muslim's office. Two
Muslim students were standing next to their office, so I
boldly addressed all three of them, "Do you believe that
prophets tell the truth?"

One answered, "Yes, of course a prophet tells the truth."

"Do you know what Jesus said about Himself?"

No answer.

So I asked, "Have you read the New Testament?"

"No."

They were being polite and soft-spoken. So I answered in turn, "That's the trouble with you guys. You say you believe in Jesus, but if you have not read the New Testament, I wonder if you really know the truth about Him."

Then they began firing questions at me. "How do you know the Bible is true?"

"Because of all the prophecies that have been fulfilled. For example, Jesus told His disciples at least three times that He would be crucified, and buried... and on the third day He would rise from the dead."

"But how do you know that's true?" one of them asked.

So I gave them my favorite illustration: "It's just plain common sense. Suppose I say to you: 'I am a prophet. Now watch. Do you see that wall? I will now walk right through it." I take three steps toward the wall and... BUMP!

"So now, do you think I am a prophet? Of course not— you would know I am either a liar or I'm crazy! Think about it. If Jesus did not rise from the dead as He said He would; if His disciples never again saw Him alive, He and everything He said would have lost all credibility—and that would have put an end to the Christian faith!"

"In fact, two days after the crucifixion, His disciples had gone back to their former occupation—fishing. But, on the third day, when they saw the Living Christ, and the Holy Spirit came to them on the day of Pentecost, they became on fire to preach the Gospel. The Gospel is Good News—that Jesus died to take away the sins of the world for everyone that would put their trust in Him."

One threw another question at me—something about justice—that I didn't understand. Glancing at my watch, I said, "I'm sorry fellows, I'd love to answer your questions, but right now I have to go to the Bible Study."

Since I only knew of one person who planned to come, I threw caution to the wind and continued, "You guys are welcome to come... and I will try to answer your questions there. We meet in conference room 5."

Guess what? Two of them came with me and five minutes later the other one walked in. (I'll refer to them here as X, Y, and Z). Stephanie and another Christian named Tilden were already there. So it was three of them against three of us—more than fair with God on our side.

After introductions and passing out Bibles, I led in a short prayer, thanking God for each one who came, and asking for His wisdom and blessing on the study, in the name of our precious Lord and Savior, Jesus Christ. Then I said again, "If you have any more questions, I will try to answer them according to the Bible."

They did! "What about Hitler? What about the KKK?"

Oh I love these kinds of questions. They give such a perfect opportunity to talk about the love of God. So I said, "Neither Hitler nor the KKK were Christians. In fact, they were directly opposed to our beliefs." I continued, "The Bible makes it clear that God created Adam and Eve and everyone descended from them. Therefore, we are all equal. But Hitler believed the Germans were a super race—and he put to death millions of Jews whom he said contaminated the German race.

The Ku Klux Klan stirred up hatred against African-Americans and cruelly persecuted them just because they were black. There is no way they could be called Christian! They just took a few verses from scripture out of context and distorted the meaning to serve their own evil purposes."

Jesus said, "*I give unto you a new commandment. Love one another even as I have loved you.*" (John 13:34) Then He demonstrated His love for us by dying on the cross to pay for our sins. (Romans 5:8) He loves all peoples regardless of race or color."

They were ready with many more questions. "Why are there so many translations of the Bible? How do you know which translation is the best?"

The Holy Spirit put this answer in my mind: "The Bible is still the best-selling book in the world and many publishers want to get a piece of the action. To comply with copyright laws, they must change a certain percentage of the wording. That's the main reason there are so many different translations on the market today. The words are different, but basically, they all say the same thing."

This started a big discussion about all the various translations, so inevitably Muslim X asked me if I had ever read the Qur'an. I told him I had read a condensed version that I picked up here at the college. So now, it was my turn to ask a question. "I've heard that the Qur'an tells Muslims to kill Christians and Jews. Is that true? And what about the terrorists?"

Muslim Y said, "The Qur'an doesn't teach that. It's just like you said with KKK: some people interpret the Qur'an wrong and distort the teachings. We do not believe the terrorists are true Muslims."

(I have learned that there are two different versions of the Qur'an: one that they read, and another they offer us to read. But I knew it would not profit anything to argue that with them.)

Muslim Z had another question. "Why do you say Jesus was the Son of God?"

"Let's turn to John 3:16," I replied. We read the verse together. "Here Jesus is saying He is the only begotten Son"

Tim joined in: "So did Peter. Remember when Jesus asked His disciples, '*Who do you say that I am?*' Peter answered, '*Thou art the Christ, the Son of the Living God.*' (Matthew 16:16)

I felt it was time to begin a structured study, so I interjected, "Today, let's begin our study in the Gospel of John, Chapter one." With Tim's help, they all turned to it— Praise God! We read the first 14 verses... all about "...*in the beginning was the Word; the Word was with God, and the Word was God; created everything... Then the Word became flesh and dwelt among us...*"

This started a big discussion about the trinity; so I took them to Genesis 1:26 where God said, "*Let us make man in our image...*" (Although they say they read the Torah, that was new to them.) I explained that "*us*" and "*our*" referred to God-the Father; God-the Son; and God-the-Holy Spirit.

That lead to another great question: Muslim Y asked, "Well if Jesus was God, why did He pray to God?"… "Yeah, like in the Lord's prayer?" questioned Muslim X.

Stephanie jumped in with the answer: "The disciples asked the Lord to teach them how to pray. So He taught them what we call the Lord's Prayer as a model of how to pray."

Muslim Z was ready with the best question of all, "OK, but how about when Jesus prayed from the cross, *"Father, why hast thou forsaken me?"* (Mark 15:34)

I jumped on that one like a big dog—explaining that "Jesus was always in communication with His Father… He only did that which His Father showed Him to do. However when Jesus hung on the cross, He had become sin for us… the sins of the whole world had been laid on him—like the scapegoat in Leviticus 16—so now, for the first time in His life, He did not feel the presence of God. Because God hates sin, sin separates us from God. That's why Jesus said, *"Verily, verily, I say unto you, except a man be born again, he can not see the kingdom of God."* (John 3:3)

Muslim Z (just like Nicodemus) said, "What's it mean—to be born again?" Praise God!

We were running out of time, so I shared the short version of my own testimony: how I was wonderfully born again at age 29, when I asked God to take control of my life and… how the Holy Spirit gave me the power and the desire to live a life that was pleasing to God. (My complete testimony appears in chapter 17.)

I then gave all of them Bibles and they promised to read the Gospel of John if I agreed to read some of their literature.

Well students, we learned some questions that Muslims ask to undermine the faith of weak Christians. And we can praise God for using three members of His Body that day to share the love of Jesus and be a testimony for His Glory.

*   *   *

Epilogue

Near the end of the semester, Muslim "W" came to our Bible study again. I remembered him from last year at one of the first sessions we had. He came in late after the last student had just shared a short testimony. I thought he was a Christian, so I invited him to share his testimony also. After he talked about a minute, I realized he was preaching Muslim stuff—so I politely said, "Excuse me my friend, we are here to study the Bible, and what you are saying is opposed to our beliefs, so we can't allow you to continue. However, you are welcome to stay, and I personally would like to get better acquainted with you. Let's have a cup of coffee together soon, okay?" He nodded in agreement and became silent for the rest of the meeting. However, he listened intently.

After we closed the meeting with prayer, surprisingly, he gave me a big hug on his way out. I think he sensed the love of God in that meeting.

Something he had said made me realize that Muslims thought America was a Christian nation—and they judged Christianity by our culture. To correct that impression, I wrote him a three-page letter, spelling out what it really means to be a Christian—and the next time I saw him, I gave him the letter.

He came to another study near the end of the semester and just quietly listened to the discussion. About two weeks later, he came to our table and picked up several tracts. We were occupied talking with someone else, so he walked away before we had an opportunity to talk with him. I sensed that he was sincerely searching for the truth, and we began to pray earnestly for him.

The following week, God brought only one person to the study. You guessed it—it was "W." God gave us the words that "W" needed to hear, and I shared my conversion experience—including my prayer to give God control of my life. He asked me to write the prayer down for him. I wrote it down. He read it. Then he put his head down and silently prayed. When he looked up, wiping tears from his cheek, he said, "I have been searching for the truth for six years and I finally found it."

"W" just became our brother in Christ. Oh what a day of rejoicing that was!

*   *   *

What do you say to a DOCTOR?

I bet the medical profession is a very satisfying one. It must be wonderful to be able to help people when they are sick and in pain. I wonder—do you know the greatest doctor that ever lived? He healed those who were blind, deaf, crippled, and had all manner of illnesses—even leprosy—just by the touch of His hand. I guess you know I'm talking about Jesus. Do you have a personal relationship with Him?

CHAPTER 7

In the Neighborhood

But sanctify the Lord God that is in your hearts, and be
ready always to give answer to every man that asks you a
reason for the hope that is in you...

1 PETER 3:15

A Divine Appointment at a Gas Station

The Lord has always blessed me with great fellowship, and
for several months I met with Tom Yoakum (a former
missionary with New Tribes Mission) for breakfast and
prayer together. One of the things we usually prayed is for
the Holy Spirit to open up divine appointments for us to be a
witness. As always, He makes these appointments at times
and places that we least expect.

When I was in line, waiting my turn outside of the
men's room at a gas station, a car pulled up to the curb and
the driver jumped out and stood next to me to wait his turn.
He was young—probably early twenties—and very well
dressed. Without exaggerating, his car was absolutely one of
the most beautiful vehicles that I had ever seen. I thanked
God for providing this natural way to open a conversation.

"Man, that is one cool set of wheels!" I exclaimed,
"Wow! That is ab-so-lute-ly beautiful! What make is it?"

He lit up a cigarette and happily told me all about it.

But time was running short, so after a little more car
chit-chat, I jumped right in with a serious question: "Tell me,
my friend, are you building up any treasures in Heaven?"

He took another puff on his cigarette and then surprised
me by saying, "Oh sure. I go to church every Sunday. My
father is a preacher. So was my grandfather. All my family is
Christian."

Although I believed he was saved, the fact that he

smoked indicated to me that he may not be enjoying a close walk with the Lord. I've been there myself—separated from God by a big smoke screen—so I am always grieved to see a professing Christian smoking. Because I know how difficult it is to break free from this addiction, I look for opportunities to testify how God delivered me. Or I give them a paper that I wrote on the subject, which includes the Gospel. (See Appendix 1.)

The restroom never became available—because God pro-vided time for me to share the word this man needed. After brief introductions, I said to him, "George, I doubt if you would ever put kerosene in the gas tank of your beautiful car would you?"

"Of course not." he replied.

"Would you drive 50,000 miles without getting an oil change?"

"No way."

"I know you love your car... you probably take excellent care of it. And, no doubt, it cost a bundle of money. But that is nothing, compared to the incredible cost Jesus paid for our salvation... so that our lives will give glory to God."

Praise the Lord; George listened, as I briefly told him how God delivered me from smoking after I promised Him, "...I will never put a cigarette in my mouth again as long as I live."

Before parting, we joined hands and prayed together, "Lord Jesus, we know your Word says our body is a Holy Temple. Please help us to keep our bodies pure and healthy for your name's sake."

Then we both raced down the road to look for another public restroom.

*   *   *

...And Jesus said unto her,
"Neither do I condemn thee; go, and sin no more."

Heavenly Conversation at McDonald's

I was lingering over my second cup of coffee one morning and enjoying my big black car-Bible that was open on the table in front of me, when a pale, sickly looking little man approached me. He stood quietly in front of me until I noticed him, then he earnestly asked me a question: "Pardon me, but do you believe in heaven?"

"Oh yes, absolutely, certainly I believe in heaven!" I said. "Why do you ask?"

"Because I am dying," he replied sadly.

I motioned to the seat across from me and said, "Please have a seat, my friend. What makes you think you're dying?"

"I have terminal cancer," he stated flatly.

"Well, I know many people who have been cured of cancer." I started to tell him about a friend of mine...

But he interrupted and said, "I also am HIV positive." He pointed to a man sitting nearby, and said, "He is my friend. He stays with me and takes good care of me."

I didn't want to hurt him, but in order to be of any help to him, I felt that I had to know, so I inquired as gently as possible, "Are you homosexual?"

"Yes, but I haven't practiced that behavior for several years."

"Well, thank God for that! I guess you know that the Bible states that it is a grievous sin and an abomination to God. However, there is no sin so terrible that God will not forgive!" I opened my Bible to 1 John and let him read for himself verse 1:9, which says *"If we confess our sins, He is faithful and just to forgive us our sins and cleanse us from all unrighteousness."*

52

Further conversation convinced me that he truly had been born again and had repented from his sins. He was, however, afraid of dying and needed more assurance that heaven was a real place, so in addition to sharing 1 Corinthians 2:9 *"Eye hath not seen, nor ear heard, neither have entered into the heart of man, the things that God hath prepared for them that love Him,"* along with many other scriptures that refer to heaven, I told him the following story that has been told many times by my relatives:

Sarah was the youngest daughter in my dad's family of five girls and four boys. Ever since she was just a little tot, it seemed God had His hand on her in a special way. She simply loved to go to Sunday school, hear Bible stories, and sing songs about Jesus! But sad to say, when Sarah was 12 years old, she became critically ill with some disease that was incurable in those days. Although she was very weak and confined to bed for many days toward the end of her life, she always seemed to be happy and content.

One afternoon, she asked everyone to come to her room because she wanted to tell them something. When everyone gathered around her bed, she said something like this:

"I know I will be leaving here soon, and I don't want anyone to worry about me. Last night I just saw a little peek of a beautiful place where I will be going to live. It must have been heaven, cause I saw Grandpa... and angels... and everybody was so happy. And I heard the most beautiful music I ever heard, and colors like I never saw before! So I don't want anybody to feel sorry for me when I die."

Sarah died peacefully in her sleep that very night.

God used Sarah's testimony to strengthen the faith of everyone in her family. And I thank God that I've had occasions to share it with many folks, including the sad man at McDonalds. I believe it comforted him.

*   *   *

*Walk in wisdom toward them that are without,
redeeming the time. Let your speech be always with grace,
seasoned with salt, that you may know
how to answer every man.*

COLOSSIANS 4:5-6

Jesus Ran the Table

An interesting assortment of characters usually hangs out in the poolroom at the Senior Citizen's Center near my home in Bowie, Maryland. Once in a while, I enjoy dropping by for a couple of hours to show off my skills at the billiard tables. I confess it's a sign of a misspent youth—but it's a lot of fun! No gambling allowed—just good-natured kibitzing, creative insulting, and bull-shooting. Some are better bull-shooters than pool shooters. And best of all: it's free for senior citizens—and provides many opportunities for witnessing.

One morning, five or six men were there when I walked in. Immediately, one fellow who was an outspoken skeptic of Christianity and a dedicated agitator, called out, "Here comes that religious fanatic."

Suddenly everyone became quiet to hear my answer.

"No, my friend," I said very clearly, "I'm not religious, and I'm not a fanatic. I just love the Lord, and I walk and talk with Him. That's normal. That's what Adam and Eve did, until they disobeyed God and ate the forbidden fruit. Then they hid from God. That's what most people do today. And that's a darn shame!"

Another time, someone asked me, "Does God help you make those tough shots, and help you win games?"

"Sure," I said, "God helps me do everything! Win or lose, I depend on Him for every breath I take."

The Lord has given me several opportunities to share the whole Gospel with friends in the poolroom.

*   *   *

Pray without ceasing. In everything give thanks:
for this is the will of God in Christ Jesus concerning you.

Tournament Time

Another day in the same poolroom, the annual eight-ball tournament was about to begin. I had signed up to play with fifteen other contenders. Although the atmosphere is usually congenial, often during a tournament, things become somewhat tense. Arguments could develop about the legality of certain shots, etc.

I was acquainted with most of the people, and I knew that there were at least two other Christians there—and most of them knew that John Thrift was a Christian. Suddenly I felt a leading of the Holy Spirit to say, "Would it be OK with everyone if we asked John to lead us in a prayer before we begin?"

For a moment, no one said a word, and then someone else spoke up, "Would anyone be offended?" Again, no answer. So I said to John, "John, will you please lead us in a prayer?"

John was ready! He thanked God for the place, the good times we have shooting pool—and then he thanked God for the salvation we have in Jesus Christ!

What a difference the Lord can make in a poolroom! Not only was the tournament great fun, but also I met three more Christians that day! Incidentally, John won the 1st prize.

Epilogue

Now, the best of the story: I was so impressed with the boldness of John's prayer, that later, I asked him if he would like to join with me to teach a Bible study once a week at Prince George's Community College. He welcomed the opportunity. In fact, he said he had been praying that God would open a new door of ministry for him. He has proven to be a terrific witness and Bible teacher every Thursday at the college...up until the time of this writing.

*   *   *

If any man be in Christ, he is a new creature: old things are passed away; Behold, all things are become new.

2 CORINTHIANS 5:17

Visitation Frustration

Larry, our church's outreach director in the 1990's, learned of some folks who had recently moved into the neighborhood near our church in Adelphi, Maryland... so we decided to welcome them and look for an opportunity to share the gospel. After some prayer for God to prepare the way, we knocked on the door. A smart-alecky little kid and a huge killer dog—jumping and barking in a most unfriendly manner—greeted us.

Finally, a big guy with arms covered with tattoos and a beer can in hand came to the door. We shouted our introductions and asked if he would have time for a short visit. He called off the wild beast, invited us to come in, and offered us a beer.

I said with a grin, "No thanks. My mother says I am too young to drink." (I was 60 years old at the time.) He chuckled and introduced us to everyone. Then he went back to the kitchen and brought in a couple of chairs for us.

The small combination living/dining room was crowded with stacks of unpacked boxes along one wall. Everybody was friendly enough, except for two of the four children, who were fighting for the possession of some toy—perfectly illustrating the fact that we are all born with a sin nature. Four adults were sitting around the table while some man was apparently explaining an insurance policy; and some scruffy-looking dude with a ponytail sat on the floor watching TV.

It seemed like utter confusion. Such a noisy hubbub! The course we had been studying on soul-winning had not prepared us for this scene. However, Larry was able to engage the tattooed man in a conversation, so during the commercial, I sat on the floor next to David, the ponytail man, and used the old strategy of talking so softly he couldn't hear what I said.

Surprisingly, it worked, and he turned the TV off. After a few minutes of small talk, it was obvious that he wasn't saved, but he seemed open to discuss spiritual matters, so I began to share the *Four Spiritual Laws* tract. After sharing the first spiritual law... "God loves you and has a purpose for your life," David asked, "Does the Bible teach what the purpose of life is?"

"It sure does," I said, "Let me show you one of the verses that tells about one of God's purposes for living." I opened my pocket testament to Romans 8:28-29 and read, *"And we know that all things work together for good to them that love God, and are the called according to His purpose. For whom He did foreknow, He also did predestinate to be conformed to the image of His Son."*

I no sooner began to enlarge on this, when another knock was heard at the front door. Naturally, the faithful watchdog went into his act. A passel of old friends had come to visit. "Well I'll be a blankety-blank son-of-a-so'n-so! What a surprise! Man, it's great to see you guys! You're a sight for sore eyes!" Out came more beer and more chairs from the kitchen.

No doubt, it was party time—time for us to disappear. I left the tract on the TV, and we hurriedly said our goodbyes.

About a month later, I was sitting in a dismal looking little sandwich shop in Adelphi, eating a boring lunch. It was rainy, chilly, and gloomy—one of those days when I really did not expect anything good to happen.

I guess the Lord knew I needed a little cheering up, so

he sent a guy in to chase the gloom away. As soon as he came through the door, he saw me... and his smile lit up the whole room. While he was saying, "Hey, Warren! Am I glad to see you!" I was trying to figure out who in the world he was.

He knew I didn't recognize him, and no wonder—the last time I saw him he had a scruffy beard and a ponytail. But now he was bright-eyed, clean-shaven, short hair, and aglow with the joy of the Lord!

Refreshing my memory, he said, "You and another guy came to our house to visit us about a month ago. We had just moved into a house on Baker Street., and I asked you what was the purpose in living? You showed me some verses in the Bible in Romans, chapter 8."

He continued, "Man, I had always wondered what my purpose in living was. I've been hoping to see you again so I could thank you..."

"Well, praise the Lord! Yes, now I remember you. David, right? Sit down here and tell me what's happening, my friend."

After ordering lunch, he told me the story. Here's the condensed version: he read the Four Spiritual Laws, prayed the prayer, got acquainted with a Christian where he worked who took him to his church, and he plans to be baptized in two weeks.

He couldn't remember the name of our church, but that's okay, because God led him to a good Bible-believing church. He seemed to really have the joy of the Lord!

Hallelujah! I thought to myself, Thank you Jesus! Even during that frustrating evening, your Word cut through all the confusion, and you worked all things together for good according to your heavenly purpose.

*   *   *

Our Father who art in heaven, hallowed be thy name.

MATTHEW 5:9

God Hears Every Word

Four loud, vulgar mouths were having an animated discussion at a lunch table. Their voices could easily be heard throughout the drugstore. One of them kept bringing God into the conversation—but in a very loose way. After hearing this five or six times, I got plain sick and tired of it, so I went over to their table, and looking at the offender directly between his eyes, I offered this priceless bit of information: "Pardon me sir, but do you realize—He can hear every word you say?"

One of the brighter looking men asked, "Who can hear every word we say?"

I love questions like that. So I said, "God! And I must warn you, He does not like hearing His name used in vain. I advise you to be extremely careful how you toss His name around. It's a very serious offense and you could be in deep trouble."

Cutting this sermon very short, I made a quick exit while they were still sitting there with their mouths open, asking each other, "Who in the hell does he think he is?"

I suppose this was not the best kind of witnessing. It sure didn't convey God's love. Nevertheless, on the other hand, a great revival started years ago in New England when Jonathon Edwards preached his famous sermon entitled "Sinners in the Hands of an Angry God

I just wish I had had the presence of mind to tell them, "Believe in Jesus while there is still time, or prepare to spend eternity in the Lake of Fire."

*   *   *

Behold the Lamb of God,
which taketh away the sin of the world.

JOHN 1:29

The Holy Spirit Went to Wendy's

Hallelujah! The Lord showed me a new way for me to witness! It was a hot summer afternoon and I dropped into a Wendy's just to relax for a few minutes and to enjoy a Frosty. I began to think about a message Pastor Schuppe had preached at Belcroft Bible Church. It was about the Passover. Just thinking about it, I became excited—and a strong feeling came over me that the Lord sent me to Wendy's to talk to someone.

The room had become strangely quiet. I looked around and noticed there were only two other customers there. One was a shy-looking, middle-aged lady who glanced at me a couple of times, but somehow I didn't think it would be wise to approach her, maybe because she may misread my intentions. The other person was a young man seated on the other side of the room. He had finished eating but he continued to just sit there, as though something was troubling him. As I watched him, he absent-mindedly pushed some spilled sugar around on the table with a little card. I knew he was the one I was supposed to talk to.

I walked over and quietly stood facing him until he looked up. "Pardon me," I said, "I've been thinking about something so exciting, I would just like to share it with you. Would that be okay?"

Although his expression said, "wonder what he's selling?" he just nodded *okay* without speaking, so I pulled out a chair and sat down across from him. As near as I recall, the conversation went some thing like this: "My name is Warren. What's your name?"

After studying me a moment, he answered "Girard," and we shook hands.

This was one of those wonderful times when I felt the

presence of the Lord so clearly—I just opened my mouth and let Him do the talking: "Girard, are you familiar with the Bible story about when the Jews were slaves in Egypt... and the Lord sent Moses to talk to the Pharaoh and ask him to let my people go?"

Girard held on to his poker face and replied, "Yeah."

"And do you remember how Pharaoh refused, so God started sending all those plagues on the land?"

"Yeah." Girard's eyes were opening a little wider now, like he was starting to come out of a fog, and seemed to be encouraging me to continue.

"At first, the Lord turned all the rivers into blood; then God covered the land with frogs; another time flies; then locusts; then boils; all kinds of bad stuff kept happening— and each time Pharaoh promised Moses that if he asked God to take away these things, he would let the Israelites go. But later Pharaoh's heart became hardened and he changed his mind. Do you remember what the tenth plague was Girard?"

He thought a few moments and then answered, "All the first born sons of the Egyptians died."

"Right. Did you hear those stories in Sunday School?" I asked.

"Yeah—a long time ago."

Praise God, I thought to myself—he's getting interested, so I pressed on. "Do you remember what the Jews did so that the death angel did not kill their babies?"

"They put blood on the door-posts of their houses?" He answered as if he was asking a question.

"Yes! When the destroyer saw the blood, he passed over their houses. That's why the Jews still celebrate the Passover every year ... and they tell their children the story. Now this is what I'm so excited about: did you ever see the connection between the Passover and the crucifixion of Jesus?"

"No, not really."

"Well, let me try to explain. Okay?" He just nodded.

I had a feeling we were running out of time, so talking fast, I said, "Moses told the people to kill a lamb or a goat. It had to be a healthy animal, without blemish. Then pour the blood in a basin. He told them to dip hyssop into the basin of blood and strike both doorposts and the lintel overhead with the blood.

"Now Girard, get this picture." I stretched my arms out to picture Jesus hanging on the cross. "Do you see how the blood from the nails in Jesus' hands, and the crown of thorns on His head would stain the cross in the same configuration as the Passover blood on those doorways in Egypt? And in the same way that the blood saved the lives of those Jewish children—and caused Pharaoh to release them from slavery in Egypt—the shed blood of Jesus frees us from slavery to sin!

"As John the Baptist declared, '*Jesus is the Lamb of God that takes away the sin of the world!*' And like the Passover lambs, Jesus was without a blemish, or without sin. Isn't that awesome? And to top it off: on the exact same day as Christ was crucified, the Jews were in Jerusalem celebrating The Passover."

Girard said, "Wow! I never saw that connection. That is awesome!

I dropped my voice and asked very gently, "Do you go to church Girard?"

"No. Not very often."

"Have you been born again?" I asked.

"No."

"Well, you know Jesus said in John, chapter 3 "...*Unless you are born again, you cannot see the Kingdom of God.*" Girard, I'll be happy to explain what that means— and tell you how you can be born again, if you wish."

Girard glanced at his watch and said, "Man! I've gotta get back to work. I don't have time now. But I sure enjoyed talking to you, Warren." When he stood up, I noticed the Wendy's logo on his shirt. He worked there.

"Well, let me give you something to read that will explain it. It's in my car. I'll be right back.

"Okay" he said, and he hurried back toward the kitchen.

When I came back in, he came out of the kitchen and received my tracts and printed testimony. He thanked me with a big smile. I believe God is going to do something great with Girard. I purpose to look for him again at Wendy's.

*   *   *

Make a joyful noise unto the Lord, all ye lands.

PSALM 100:1

A Sanctified Saxophone

Every Friday and Saturday night for about three years, I played saxophone and clarinet with a swinging five-piece dance band in a small nightclub near Laurel, Maryland. Sometimes the joint really jumped, so I had a ball. What's more, I enjoyed the extra green stuff.

However, when I fell in love with Jesus, I began to feel troubled about playing in that environment. You know—booze, smoke, lights down low, pulsating rhythms, suggestive dancing, etc—were definitely not conducive to growing in the Lord. I tried to keep my mind focused on the music instead of the dancers, but I confess—I was not too successful. I even drank an occasional beer until one night when I came home and my wife, Helen, was waiting for me with about six Bible verses telling me why I should not drink the wine when it moved in the glass, etc. So from then on, I stuck to coffee and sodas.

I stuck in this mode for about six months—often praying that I would play so beautifully that it would be a testimony for God (ha ha)—and then the real test of my faith came: somebody wanted to hire the band on a weeknight for a special party. They called it a *men's smoker*.

I learned that it would be very rowdy, with strip-tease dancers and all kinds of unspeakable sleazy entertainment. They were willing to pay the band double our usual fee and they especially wanted me to play the sax! Strippers say the sax is sexy.

I thought about Psalm 23, *"He leads me in paths of righteousness for His name's sake,"* and I'm glad to report that I found I had a backbone after all and I simply refused, telling them that, as a Christian, I could not participate. That was my best witness to the band! They just could not understand how I could pass up all that extra loot, not to mention the titillation. They soon located another sax man—and it was my turning point of going from Jazz to Jesus.

These days—now that my allegiance has switched from Benny Goodman, the King of Swing to Jesus, the King of Kings—God gives me many opportunities to play for His glory. My experiences in playing jazz taught me how to improvise, so I have arranged several well-known hymns with variations for saxophone solos. These are well received in church, especially by the young people.

When playing at an assisted living home for the first time, I usually say, "You may have heard that one cannot play a saxophone with false teeth. I am here to show you that is not true. I play with false teeth. The trick is—I put my teeth in my pocket." Then—I'm not kidding—I really do put them in my pocket. That never fails to get a laugh. Senior citizens can relate to that, and for me, it's a good exercise in humility.

In between tunes, I say something like; "I'd like to offer this song as a prayer for all of us. It's called "Just A Closer Walk With You" or I might say, "I wish I could play and sing at the same time, because the words of this song says, "What a Friend We Have in Jesus."

Now for one of my fondest memories of playing in an assisted-living home: at the time, I was part of a sextet that played mostly old jazz standards and Dixieland tunes. During the intermission, I asked permission to play a solo, and I announced it this way: "Now I'm going to play a very special song for you on this old rugged saxophone. I'm sure you will recognize it.

We have a choir of angels to accompany us, but we will need your help. Of course, we can't see them now, but this room is full of angels all around us, as it says in Psalm 91.

As I play, the angels will hum the melody for a background. But they want to use your voices. That's right—they will use your voices to hum along. Okay?"

It was beautiful! And just about all forty pretty ladies (if they were still awake) wore a sweet smile as they hummed along with "The Old Rugged Cross."

I thank God for the gift of music. What a wonderful way to express His love, joy, peace... and excitement.

*   *   *

CHAPTER 8

Confrontations

Finally, my brethren, be strong in the Lord, and in the
power of His might. Put on the whole armor of God,
that ye may be able to stand against the wiles of the devil.

EPHESIANS 6:10-11

Righteous Anger Can Make a Big Difference

Our church had been studying a book by Watchman Nee entitled "Sit, Walk, and Stand." This is a wonderful study based on the book of Ephesians, which traces the pattern of growth from a babe-in-Christ to a mature Christian. In chapter 2, we begin by sitting *"...and hath raised us up together, and made us sit together with Christ in heavenly places."* (Eph.2:6)

I spent a lot of time meditating on this idea of being seated in heavenly places. Can you imagine how wonderful it will be someday to find ourselves sitting around a table having fellowship with Jesus, Peter, and John; and perhaps even Moses, Joshua, and Abraham? That will be joy unspeakable.

Next in chapters 4 and 5, we are instructed to *"...walk worthy of the vocation to which we have been called."* (Eph.4:1) That's all about behavior—*"putting on the new man, which after God is created in righteousness and true holiness"* (Eph.4:25) After walking with the Lord for some time, and learning His ways, we are given God's armor and the strength to *"...stand against the enemy,"* as we are exhorted to do in chapter 6, starting at verse 10.

Soon after doing the study, the Lord gave me a test: I was shopping in a drugstore and saw something that made me furious! Two little boys (about 8 or 9 years old) were staring at pictures of half-naked girls on the covers of

"Playboy" and other porn magazines. This trash was displayed on a stand right at the boy's eye-level!

Jesus said, *"But whosoever shall offend one of these little ones that believe in me, it were better for him that a millstone were hanged about his neck, and that he were drowned in the depth of the sea."* (Matthew 18:6)

Quickly finding the manager, I addressed him: "Sir, will you please come to the front of the store? There is something I would like to show you." He obediently followed me to the garbage rack, which was very close to several people in line at the checkout counter.

Standing back about six feet from the rack and pointing, I spoke loud enough for everyone in the store to hear: "Sir, do you see those filthy magazines? Do you realize they are in full view of little children? I just saw two little boys looking at that filth."

A hush came over the store as everyone stopped to see what was going on. I continued, "That is an offense to me! And it would be an offense to anyone who believes in the Lord Jesus!"

"Yes, sir," the manager replied very meekly, "you're right. That should not be. I apologize. I'll have them moved immediately."

"Thank you, sir," I said, and walked out.

About three days later, I returned to the scene of the crime. The offending magazines had been moved to a tall shelf behind the cashier. Only the titles were visible. I found the manager and expressed my thanks to him.

Praise the Lord! This soon became the policy in all the Peoples Drug Stores (now CVS) in the Washington, DC area.

*   *   *

It is appointed unto men once to die,
but after this the judgment.

HEBREWS 9:27

Doctrines of Men

I hope this account makes you as angry at false teachers as it made Jesus!

Just a few blocks from my house in Beltsville, a good-looking young man held out his thumb for a ride. He was going to the University of Maryland in College Park—just a five-minute ride. After exchanging our names and a few pleasantries, I encouraged him to talk about himself. I said, "Tell me George, are you married?"

"No, but I am living with a girlfriend."

He didn't seem to object to personal questions, so I pressed on, "Do you believe in God?"

"Oh sure. I go to St. Joe's every Sunday." I understood he meant St. Joseph Catholic Church in Beltsville.

We were only a couple of blocks from the college so I had to talk fast.

"Whoa... you say you believe in God; you go to church; but you are shacking up. Suppose you die while you are committing fornication? What then? Do you think you would go to heaven?"

Without a moment's hesitation, George replied, "I guess I would go to purgatory. But so what? I'm sure my parents would pray me out. I'll just have to take that chance."

We were at George's destination, and he was gone before I could respond intelligently.

I can't begin to tell you how terribly sad this experience made me. I had heard about the doctrine of purgatory before, but the evil reality of it had never hit me with such force as it did now. How many millions of people are deceived and sent to hell by this false doctrine? I stewed about it the rest of the day, and the next day I determined to do something about it! It wasn't much—but it was something.

68

The name of the priest was on a sign in front of the rectory next to the church where George attended. I found his name in the telephone book and phoned for an appointment. Since I addressed him as Reverend and didn't call him Father, (Jesus taught in Matthew 23:9, *"Call no man your father upon the earth: for one is your father which is in heaven."*) I suppose he guessed that I was not a member of his parish.

"What do you wish to talk about?"

"I met a member of your parish and I am very concerned about him."

"What is his name?" the priest asked, sounding a little impatient.

"First name is George. I didn't catch his last name. He has a serious personal problem, and I believe you can help."

"What kind of problem?" he asked.

"Like I said, sir… it's very personal … and too complicated to discuss over the phone. I would appreciate it, if you could just spare 10 or 15 minutes to visit with me at your office."

I wasn't angry at him. I actually felt sorry for him, because I realized that he too could have been deceived by church tradition—in the same way as George was. He finally agreed, somewhat reluctantly, to see me that same day. I felt a little like Martin Luther when I knocked on his door. (I'm sure grateful that they no longer burn "heretics" at the stake.)

He ushered me into his office and offered me a chair near the door. The whole wall behind his elegant chair displayed a very impressive collection of books from floor to ceiling. Trying not to feel intimidated in the presence of this highly educated doctor of divinity, I just jumped right in and related my conversation with George. Then I asked him, "Where does this idea of purgatory come from? Can you show it to me in the Bible?"

The black-robed doctor of divinity launched into a long dissertation on Greek philosophy, psychology, and history. He didn't once refer to the Bible! So I patiently asked him again, "But sir, where does this appear in the Bible?"

This man was a master at dancing all around the subject but never landing on the mark. He finally referred to some verse from 1st John that in no way referred to purgatory, and then went into another long lecture about history, philosophy, and church tradition. I let him ramble on until he got tired of talking, and then it was my turn. I started shooting questions at him rapid-fire without giving him time to answer:

"What about the verse in Hebrews that says, "...*it is appointed unto men once to die, but then comes the judgment.*" Do you realize the awesome responsibility that you have as a teacher to teach the truth? Are you willing to suffer the wrath of God if you are teaching a lie? If purgatory is nothing but a lie that was carried over from pagan religions, are you willing to teach your people lies that could send them to hell?"

That brought our meeting to an abrupt end. I believe he turned a little pale as he showed me the door. I pray that his struggle to try to justify the doctrine of purgatory will put doubts in his mind, and cause him to seek the truth.

Although this experience seemed futile at the time, praise the Lord, it taught me something useful: The Holy Bible is our absolute authority! However, unfortunately there are religions—even some that masses of people believe are Christian—that accept tradition and beliefs from other sources even if they contradict the Holy Bible. I fear they are standing on sinking sand.

*　　*　　*

Surely goodness and mercy shall follow me all the days of my life: and I shall dwell in the house of the Lord forever.

PSALM 23:6

But Forever Doesn't Mean ...Forever

Rabbi Bernstein's secretary answered the phone. I prayed the Lord would give me the words to say. "I work near here, and

I wonder if I could meet with Rabbi Bernstein on my lunch hour some day this week, say about 12:15?"

"May I tell him the purpose of your visit?"

Being careful not to be too specific, I answered, "I'd like to talk to him about a spiritual matter."

"Can you please be a little more specific?" she asked.

"Well... It's kind of complicated."

"What is your name?"

"Warren Sears"

"Are you a member of this congregation?"

"No. But I am not a salesman."

"Are you planning to marry a Jewish girl?"

Boy, this gal was nosey. "No. I am already married."

Then she said, "Is it about conversion?" Wow! Look how the Lord set that up.

"Yes—conversion," I answered, being careful not to say whose conversion.

"Fine. Please hold a minute while I check with Rabbi Bernstein."

After a short pause, she said sweetly, "Rabbi Bernstein said he would be happy to meet you. How about 12:15 next Thursday? Is that OK?"

"Yes. Thank you. I will be there."

I called Bob Young, a faithful prayer partner, to see if he could go with me on Thursday. He agreed, but he said I should do most of the talking. Bob was a dear brother in Christ who worked nearby. We had enjoyed fellowship and prayer together nearly every day at lunchtime for several months. We frequently discussed our desire to reach Jews for Christ, and thought how wonderful it would be if Rabbi Bernstein saw the light... and how he could influence hundreds of Jews. We looked at the many prophecies in scripture concerning the Messiah that were fulfilled by Jesus. Bible scholars say there were more than 300. We decided to share Isaiah 53, which details the crucifixion, and Micah 5:2 which foretells the birth of Jesus in Bethlehem.

When the secretary introduced us, Rabbi Bernstein acted so truly glad to see us we realized at once he was confused about whose conversion we had in mind. He was intelligent looking, handsome, with an office to match, and the kind of person one would immediately like. Floor-to-ceiling books decorated two walls of his spacious office, so I was impressed we were going to be dealing with a scholar of some depth. I kept silently praying for wisdom.

He opened the conversation with: "Gentlemen, how can I help you?"

"Rabbi Bernstein," I answered, "I'm not Jewish. But all my life I've had a lot of Jewish friends; personal friends during school days; businessmen that I worked with; musicians. My teenage idol was Benny Goodman." Just to lighten things up, I said, "By the way, I still think he was the greatest clarinet player that ever lived."

He playfully interrupted, "Better than Artie Shaw?"

"Absolutely. Shaw was great, but Benny was better. I know because I used to play a clarinet myself." We both laughed about that old debate that had never been settled.

"No kidding." he said, "You know, I took a few clarinet lessons too, but I decided that the world only needed one Benny Goodman. So... here I am at your service. What can I do for you?"

"Well Sir, personally we're doing okay. But like I was saying, I have always felt a special love for Jewish people— not just because of good friends who were Jewish, but, I've read how throughout history, in spite of terrible persecution, the Jews risked their lives to protect the Holy Scriptures."

"Yes. This is true." he agreed.

"Now," I continued, "the thing I can't understand—why so many young Jews today, even though they attend synagogue regularly, don't seem to have the reality of God in their life."

"Yes. Sorry to say, this is also true. You know the old saying about leading a horse to water. We try to instill the wisdom of God into them, but I'm afraid, like most people today, they are so concerned about filling up their houses with a lot of stuff they don't need, they don't have time to think about spiritual things."

"You got that right," I responded. "But there's something else. For example, let me tell you about a Jewish man that I work with. We've talked some about personal things. Even though he and his wife celebrate Jewish Holy days, I'm beginning to realize that, for them, the Holy days do not have any reality. For example, Larry and I were having lunch together one day and he frankly told me, "My wife and I celebrate the Passover—although we don't really believe the stories about Moses and the plagues in Egypt are true. It's just our tradition.

"That really puzzled me, so after thinking about it for a couple minutes, I said, 'Larry, do you believe in that peach that you're eating? Then surely you must believe in peach trees. The point I'm trying to make—where something actually exists, their must be a real source for its existence. Larry wasn't convinced... and sir, it really saddens me to realize that so many Jewish people today have no faith in God's promises. They have no hope of eternal life in heaven; no fear of hell; and like the rest of the world, they love to party, smoke dope, and drink booze."

Now the rabbi was beginning to look a little uncomfortable, but he patiently responded, "Eternal life is not in our scriptures."

"What about the 23rd Psalm?" I asked.

"What verse?" he snapped.

"The last verse, *Surely goodness and mercy shall follow me all the days of my life, and I shall dwell in the house of the Lord forever.*"

The rabbi turned up the volume a little and declared, "Forever doesn't mean forever. The trouble is you guys have translations that are not true to the original."

I think he was starting to catch on about whose conversion we had in mind. So, very meekly, I asked, "What does forever mean?"

"It means for as long as you are living."

"Really?" I was confused. I was at a loss for words.

His friendly expression darkened and he said, very pointedly, "Exactly why did you men come here today?"

I thought a moment before answering. This was the moment of truth—probably the last chance to share the gospel with Rabbi Bernstein, so I said something to this effect.

"When I was 29 years old, I was going through an emotional crisis and was struggling with the same kind of doubts that my Jewish friends do, and someone asked me if I knew the 23rd Psalm. The fact is, when I was just a little child, I had been taught to memorize it. That night, driving alone in my car on a country road, I began thinking about it. The images it brought to mind gave me such peace... green pastures...still waters... paths of righteousness... just what I needed. I said to myself, 'This is so beautiful, maybe it really is the Word of God as some people say it is.'

"I pulled my car off the road and prayed, 'God, if you are real, I want you to take control of my life. I am tired of living my way. I put my life in your hands.' Then I went home and went to bed.

"The next day I was a different person with a whole new outlook on life. I fell in love with God and the people that He brought into my life. I had peace and joy that I never knew before. Scripture became alive to me and I learned that Isaiah 53 was a prophecy of the Messiah. We call Him Jesus. The Good Shepherd in Psalm 23 is Jesus..."

That did it! Rabbi Bernstein leaped out of his chair and shouted. "YOU HAVE DECEIVED ME. YOU HAVE DECEIVED ME. HOW DARE YOU DECEIVE ME?" Then he howled and screamed at his secretary, WHY? HOW? WHAT?..." His words drowned out anything else we might try to say, as he practically pushed us out the door.

As we look back on that, I wonder: did the Lord really set that up? Or was it the devil? The Rabbi may not have become so angry if I had just stuck to my original request to talk with him about a spiritual matter... instead of *conversion.*

Bob and I both wrote him a follow-up letter, mainly thanking him for his time, apologizing for allowing the deception, and incidentally, referencing a couple more prophecies of the Messiah.

Sorry to say, we never heard from him again.

*   *   *

For they loved the praise of men
More than the praise of God.

JOHN 12:43

A Transgressor in the Camp

This happened a few years ago when I belonged to another church which—to protect it from further embarrassment—I would rather not identify. It was not a joy! But sometimes we just gotta do what we gotta do. It's all part of living the Christian life. When God puts a heavy burden on your heart and makes it clear what you should do, He will give you no rest until you just say "Amen Lord," and go do it.

For several months I had been disturbed about a church member who always parked in a highly visible place in front of the church with a religious symbol on the license tag that identified him as a member of an organization that clearly teaches that salvation can be earned by doing good works... as well as many other things that are opposed to the gospel according to Jesus.

My concern about this cult member (I'll call him Fred) deepened when our church set a goal to evangelize everyone within a three-mile radius... and they appointed me to be the evangelism director. I considered this to be an awesome responsibility and spent much time in prayer about it. I knew we had to be prepared for spiritual warfare.

God teaches us a powerful lesson in Joshua, chapter three, showing how one man, Achan, disobeyed God and caused Israel to lose the battle of Ai. I think this principle holds true in the battle to win souls to Christ. One sinner in the camp can greatly hinder the work of the Holy Spirit. And

75

if we go out as a team to intentionally share Christ without the unity and the power of the Holy Spirit on our side, Satan can make us look like fools.

At the same time, something else happened that convinced me that God was leading me to confront this issue: I was invited to attend a weekly lunch meeting with Christians from various ministries who just met for fellowship and prayer. Although I never spoke a word to anyone at these meetings about my concern with the cult member, one day a woman brought three books to the table and offered to loan them to me. They were written by former members of the same organization that Fred belonged to. These books, along with the "Encyclopedia of Cults and New Age Religions" by John Ankenberg, convinced me this was indeed a false religion that needed to be dealt with.

I tried to convince the pastor and elders about the seriousness of this matter, but no one was willing to confront good ol' Freddie. After much prayer and further procrastination on my part—I did not relish doing this—I felt I was being led to speak to Fred according to what Jesus taught in Matthew 18:15-17. So I called him and made an appointment to meet with him the following Monday.

Interestingly, when I awoke Monday morning, the Lord put the story of David and Bathsheba on my mind—the part where the Lord sent Nathan to confront David about his sin (II Samuel 12:1-8). This gave me the idea of how to broach the subject to Fred.

Before leaving home, I called my prayer partner and asked him to lift the meeting up in prayer. I went with high hopes that we could reason together; that perhaps Fred was not fully aware of the facts concerning the brotherhood (as he called it), and that he would reconsider his relationship to Christ and the church.

Just to break the ice, I attempted to make some small talk about his beautiful house and yard, but he was impatient to get to the point.

"This is strictly a confidential matter between you and me," I began. "I only came as a brother at my own volition;

and I was not sent by the church in some official capacity. You are probably familiar with the passage in Matthew 18 where Jesus taught, *"If thy brother shall trespass against thee, go and tell him his fault between thee and him alone; if he shall hear thee, thou hast gained thy brother."*

"Right," he said. "I know the passage."

Then I asked, "What if you knew of a man in our church who apparently has been married for years, yet occasionally he spends the night with another woman. What do you think should be done about it?"

His answer was biblically correct. "Someone who knows the man well should meet with him in private; tell him he knew what was going on, and try to persuade him to repent from his sin and get right with God."

I agreed. Then I asked him, "Do you understand what it means to commit spiritual fornication?"

"Not exactly."

"Then let me explain. The church is the bride of Christ. If a Christian worships another God besides Christ, that is spiritual fornication. I didn't think you would understand Fred, because that's what you do every time you attend a meeting of the organization you advertise by that emblem on your license plate."

At that point, things got ugly! Fred got angry; said I didn't know what I was talking about; threw papers on the floor that I brought to show him; and ordered me to leave his property.

"Okay, I'll leave," I said. "I've carried out step one, according to Matthew 18:15. Step two will come later when I shall come back with one or two witnesses."

"Well you can tell the deacons that it will be no use coming here. I will not talk to them."

Later that afternoon, he stomped up to the church and barked at the pastor. I don't know all that transpired. I was only told that he was raging mad and his final word was, "As long as Warren Sears is in this church, I will not attend."

After further discussion with the church leaders, I learned they were still unwilling to take a stand against the cult, I knew it was time for me to move on. I told the pastor, "I need a church where the leaders love the praise of God more than the praise of men. And I need a church where someone will love me enough to correct me if I stray from the truth."

Two weeks later, I found a church just four blocks away —and it's still faithful to God's Word. Thank you Jesus!

*   *   *

CHAPTER 9

Hitchhikers

For He shall give thee angels charge over thee.
to keep thee in all thy ways.

PSALM 91:11

Captive Audiences

Thanks be to God, He assigns angels to protect us. Therefore, I have no fear of picking up hitchhikers. For many years, as I drove about 30 miles each way to work and back, this became my favorite way to reach the lost. When I started up the car each morning, I often prayed, "Lord, please put someone out there today that needs to hear about Jesus. And fill me with thy Holy Spirit. Prepare my heart to be an effective witness."

After stopping to pick someone up, I would first introduce myself, ask them their name, and no matter how repulsive they looked or smelled, I'd shake hands and say, "I'm glad to meet you." Then I could address them by name. Next, I would inquire how far they were going—so I could gauge how much time I had to explain the gospel. This could vary from two minutes to forty minutes.

Of course, no two people are alike, so I always prayed for wisdom and discernment to know how to share with each individual. I learned that the way I shared with a person yesterday may not be effective to a person today. However, I learned that most hitchhikers have a few things in common that can put them in a very receptive frame of mind to listen to the gospel. They are unsettled and going through changes in their lives that could make them feel very insecure.

Often, they are running away from someone or something, such as a broken relationship with friends, family, sweetheart, etc. They're usually getting out of town and have little money, or—obviously—they would have their own car, or they would ride a bus. So in reality, they are going to begin a new life to some degree. What better time to share the new life we have in Christ?

Consider these facts as well: **1.** They are usually grateful for my giving them a ride. **2.** They are a captive audience. **3.** The standard soul-winner's question: "If you died today, are you sure that you would go to heaven?" seems timely and meaningful when you are traveling 65 miles an hour in rush-hour traffic on an Interstate Highway. However, that is not always the best approach.

If time allows, ask questions. Show that you are genuinely interested in them. Perhaps you could ask, "What kind of work do you do? Are you married? Do you have any children? Etc." Naturally, the more you can get them to talk about themselves, the better rapport you can establish, and the better you will understand how to meet their needs. Often you can give them some down-to-earth practical advice about getting suitable employment, or other worldly concerns, as well as explaining how they can have the unspeakable joy of knowing Jesus as Lord and Savior. Tell them what Jesus did for you, and how He can do the same for them.

When I know it's a short ride, I like to use a direct approach. For instance, the guy might say, "Thanks a lot for giving me a lift." I might reply, "You are very welcome! I would really like to help you get a free ride to heaven when your time on this planet is up! What do you know about the Bible? Did you know that Jesus said, "Unless you are born again, you cannot see the Kingdom of God?" That usually gets the conversation going full speed ahead.

Does this ministry bear fruit? You bet. After doing this for about a year without actually seeing any life-changing decisions for Christ, I became somewhat discouraged. So one morning I told the Lord how I felt, and I asked Him to please let me see some fruit if He wanted me to continue picking up hitchhikers. Well, thank you Lord Jesus! That very day I had two people—one in the morning on the way to work, and another in the evening on the way home—who both prayed to receive Jesus as Lord and Savior. Hallelujah!

Of course, when you deal with hitchhikers, you seldom ever see them or hear from them again. However, there are exceptions. One in particular comes to mind:

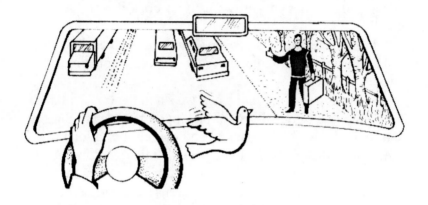

On the Way to Church

It was Sunday night one November and I was on my way to church. I picked up a young man, who said he was walking home to Upper Marlboro, a nearby town in Maryland. Feeling full of the joy of the Lord that night, I gave him a five-minute testimony and told him how happy I was to be going to church that night. I said, "I wish you could know the love, joy and peace that comes when King Jesus comes into your life."

When we got as far as the church (Riverdale Baptist), it was getting dark and pretty chilly to be out walking five more miles to his house. So I said, "James, it's getting dark and it's going to be tough for you to hitch a ride now. If you can take time to go to church with me tonight—it only lasts about an hour and a half—I promise, right after church, I will drive you home—right to your door." James agreed.

Pastor R. Herbert Fitzpatrick was in fine form and he preached the gospel with power that night. As it usually happens in most Baptist churches, at the end of the service, the pastor invited those who wished to receive Christ as Lord and Savior to come to the altar. I could see that James was struggling with the devil. So, nudging him gently, I whispered, "James, if you want to go up, I'll walk up with you."

Praise the Lord. James stood up and walked down the aisle with me beside him. Jesus was waiting for him at the altar.

Later, I drove him home and we sat in the car and talked for about a half hour. I started picking him up every Sunday and took him to Sunday school and church. For a long time, James thought of me as his spiritual father and frequently called me when he had questions about spiritual matters. A few weeks later he got baptized, purchased a car, and began bringing some friends to church with him.

But, eventually, a couple of Sundays passed and James didn't show up. I phoned him to see if he was okay. He told me that some guy where he worked persuaded him to come to his church. He was a Jehovah's Witness. I wasn't quite sure how to deal with that then, so I just told him that I would be praying for him, and we cut the conversation short.

Soon after that, I found a booklet entitled "Another Gospel" which was written by a former Jehovah's Witness, and I went to see James. I said, "James, I'd like you to do me a favor. I read this booklet, but I don't know whether it's true or not, because I've never been involved before with Jehovah's Witnesses. Would you please read this and tell me what you think?" He agreed to read it.

A few days later he phoned me and said, "Warren, I believe every word of it is absolutely true and I am getting out of it."

Praise the Lord for that booklet!

*   *   *

CHAPTER 10

Visiting Jesus in Jail

Then shall the King say unto them...
Come ye blessed of my Father, inherit the Kingdom
prepared for you from the foundation of the world;... For I
was in prison and you came unto me.

MATTHEW 10:34-36

Behind Bars and Back to Basics

Can you possibly imagine how a man would feel, knowing that just five days ago... he got drunk... backed his car into his driveway... and accidentally ran over his dear wife. She died on the way to the hospital. Now he fears that his three children hate him, and will never forgive him for killing their mother.

Now he's behind bars in a 6 x 8 cell, waiting for trial. Every time he lies down on the bunk, the whole scene plays out again before his eyes. He can't sleep without having nightmares. Most of the time, he just paces back and forth in the cell. He's sick to death of living—and afraid of dying.

That's the scenario in one man's life whom the Lord sent me to minister to one day, at the Jennifer Road Detention Center in Annapolis, Maryland.

As I walked down a narrow walkway outside of a row of cellblocks, he called out to me, "Please sir, can I talk to you?"

I suppose he saw my Good News Mission Volunteer ID badge. "Sure Man. That's why I'm here. What do you want to talk about?" I asked.

"I don't have any peace. Will you pray for me?"

He looked so pitiful, I knew only the Lord could help him. "Sure, I will pray for you," I said. "What's your name?"

"Charles."

I stuck my hand through the bars and we shook hands. I

said, "Glad to meet you Charles. My name is Warren. Well, Charles, I can tell you this for sure. The only way you can ever have any real peace in this world is by trusting the Lord Jesus. Are you a Christian?" I asked.

"Yes," he said.

"When were you born-again?"

"I was baptized about three years ago."

He also mentioned the name of the church, and I couldn't help thinking that either he has had some false teaching, or he has never really understood the gospel. I felt I needed to take him back to basics, in order to build his confidence in God's Word, so I said, "It's good you were baptized. However, being baptized is something you do after you are born again. Do you know what Jesus meant when He said you must be born again?"

"Not really," he answered.

"May I show you in the Bible what it means?"

"Yes."

I opened my Bible to John 3:3 and held it up close to the bars so he could see. I asked him to read it aloud. He read it okay, so I elaborated on the text. "Notice that Jesus told this to Nicodemus—a ruler of the Jews—a man of authority: a man who was highly respected. He said we were all born of the flesh, but we must be born of water and Spirit or we cannot even see the Kingdom of Heaven. Notice the word "Spirit" has a capital "S"—that means the Holy Spirit. When you see the word "spirit" in the Bible with a small "s," it signifies the human spirit."

Just like Nicodemus, Charles said, "How can I be born again?"

No doubt, Charles was ready, so I wanted to make sure he really understood this time. I said, "I will explain that, but first, let explain why Jesus said you must be born again. Look at the first chapter in the Bible, Genesis Chapter 1."

He had a Gideon Bible that the chaplain had given him. First I showed him how God created the whole world and everything in it... pointing particularly to verses 4, 10, 12,18, 21.where God reviewed each step in the creation and saw that *it was good.*

Then with hand gestures, I depicted the earth just floating inside a big bubble—this was marvelous—the wall of water out there in space protected the earth from the infrared rays that cause people to age. Remember, before the flood people lived to be hundreds of years old. In Genesis 5:27, we read that Methuselah lived to be 969 years old. Moses lived 950 years.

The environment was perfect the year-round—it's called the canopy effect. Imagine—there were no violent weather conditions such as tornadoes, floods, earthquakes, volcanoes, and ice storms. The temperature probably stayed around 68 degrees. It was paradise—a perfect place to live. The vegetables and fruit would have been delicious.

Then I expounded on the meaning of verse 26, where God said, *"Let us make man in our image, after our likeness..."* I asked Charles, "Do you know what God meant by our image and our likeness?"

"Was He talking about angels?" he said.

"No. Angels are created beings that God designed to be ministering servants to us. We were not made in the image of angels. God was referring to the Father, the Son, and the Holy Spirit. That's what we call *the Trinity.* So Charles, we need to understand, according to that, when God created us, He gave us a body, a soul, and a spirit. You know what the body is. The soul is your mind and your emotions. Your human spirit is the organ God gave you to receive His Holy Spirit. That's what Jesus was talking about when He said you must be born again—this happens when the Holy Spirit comes into our human spirit. Does that make sense to you Charles?"

"I think so," he said without much enthusiasm.

"Charles, to be born again is the greatest miracle that God is performing today. No one can understand what a wonderful miracle that is until they have experienced it for themselves. The greatest thing about it is knowing that our sins are forgiven, therefore, when we die, we will go to heaven: a perfect place where all of our deepest longings will be fulfilled."

This man was very depressed. I don't always do this when talking to a prisoner, but I asked him why he was in jail. Then he told me the horrible story about running over his wife. I felt I needed to share more basic stuff with him to give him a desire to live. But I only had about twenty minutes left.

"Wow! That's terrible. I know it's going to take a long time to get over it. But God loves you more than you can imagine, Charles, and He wants you to go on with your life! He knows exactly what happened, but He still loves you with an everlasting love. Do you know what 1 John 1:9 says?"

He shook his head—no. I asked him to turn to that in his Bible and read, *"If we confess our sins, God is faithful and just to forgive us our sins and cleanse us from all unrighteousness."*

"Charles, although running over your wife was an accident, your sin was getting drunk. And you need to confess that to God. Now according to the verse we just read, God will forgive you."

Charles said, "I know. I have confessed it. But I can't forget it."

I said, "Satan is called the great accuser of the brethren. He tempted you to get drunk. And now, he accuses you of killing your wife—and he doesn't want you to forget it. He knows as long as you feel guilty and worthless, you will not be a good testimony for the Lord. But, when you give God control of your life, you can tell Satan to take a hike in the name of Jesus, and he will have no power over you, unless you give it to him. Until you are willing to give your life to God, Satan can keep you living in misery. Even then, Satan will keep on reminding you of your sin—but, thank God, the Bible says, *"God removes our transgressions away from us, as far as the East is from the West."* (Psalm 103)

"Now Charles, I want you to see something that's very important. Turn back to Genesis, chapter 1. Look here at verse 28 '*...and God said unto them...*' and again in verse 29: '*And God said...*' I want you to see that, originally, God talked to Adam and Eve all the time. Can you imagine how wonderful that would be—to be friends with the creator of the universe, to walk and talk with God himself? That is normal. That is the way it was meant to be.

Think about this: after God put the whole universe in gear; and created everything that had life—the flowers and the trees, the birds and the bees, the beasts in the field and the fish in the seas—God's final masterpiece, His ultimate creation…was a man, just like you and me. Can you imagine how much He loved that little man? He gave him everything he needed including a wife, and then He put them in a beautiful garden with every good thing to eat. However, He told them, you can freely eat of the Tree of Life, and you will live forever. But do not eat of the Tree of Knowledge of Good and Evil or you will surely die. Well, I guess you know what happened."

Charles said. "Yeah. They listened to Satan—and ate the from the wrong tree."

"And then what?" I asked Charles.

"God kicked them out of Paradise?"

"Yes, but before that, they tried to hide from God, which is, of course, impossible. They were ashamed. That wonderful friendship with God was broken. That's exactly what happens today. When people sin or disobey God, they try to hide from God. Everyone has inherited that tendency to sin from Adam and Eve. The Bible says, *"all have sinned and come short of the Glory of God…"* (Romans 3:23). God hates sin—because sin destroys us and separates us from God. Romans 6:23 says *"The wages of sin is death (or hell) but the gift of God is eternal life.*

But the Good News is, in Romans 5:8 *"…God demonstrated His love for us by sending Christ to die for us while we were still sinners."* So there it is Charles. When Jesus died that horrible death on the cross, he paid the penalty in full for our sins. The only sin that God does not forgive is the sin of not believing in Jesus and receiving him as your Lord and Savior.

Let's look at Romans 10:9 *"…If you confess with your mouth that Jesus is Lord and believe in your heart that God raised Him from the dead you will be saved."*

I asked him some questions to make sure he understood the gospel. When I was convinced that he understood, I led him in a prayer to ask God to take control of his life... and give him that peace that passes all understanding.

As I advise all new Christians, I urged Charles to read the Bible every day and especially read the Gospel of John at least ten times. One good thing about a jail ministry, the converts have plenty of time to read the Word.

Charles asked me to please come back and see him next week. I promised to do so.

*　　*　　*

I'll share a few more details for those who are interested in a jail ministry. .

At the time of this writing, the assistant pastor of my church goes there with a team every Tuesday. They allowed me to go along as a guest speaker the first time, without the usual red tape, just to see if I would decide to continue.

Four of us rode together, enjoying fellowship on the way, and then we stopped somewhere for lunch, before going to the detention center at 1:00 o'clock.

The security is very tight. First, we sign in; then a guard checks our baggage, then we pass through metal detectors and finally, a guard opens the big steel doors with electronic controls.

The following week I completed an application and waited about three weeks while they conducted a criminal history check on me. Next, after an interview by the chaplain and attending an orientation meeting, I received a handbook for volunteers, a photo ID card, and now I am able to go every Tuesday—as a volunteer with the Good News Jail and Prison Ministry.

One of the important things I have learned since counseling with prisoners is—although many of them say they have received Jesus since they have been incarcerated, most of them usually feel that they <u>still don't have peace with God.</u>

I believe the main reason for this is: most of them have stolen from people, or have hurt people in some way, and now, behind bars, they have no opportunity for restitution and reconciliation. So I share Matthew 5:23-24. *"Therefore, if thou bring thy gift to the altar, and there you remember that thy brother has anything against you, leave there thy gift before the altar, and go thy way; first be reconciled to thy brother, and then come and offer thy gift."* I counsel them to purpose in their heart that at the first opportunity when they get out of jail, they will make amends. Until then, they could write letters asking forgiveness from those whom they have wronged. They could also make a decision to forgive those who have wronged them, and even write letters to those people conveying this.

Many prisoners feel like they have reached the end of the rope and they know they need the Lord. They have plenty of time to read the Word; talk with each other; think of a million questions to ask. When a prisoner is released, it is very important to impress upon this person the need to get involved with a good church. I give them a copy of a paper which I wrote entitled: "How to Find a Good Church." *See Appendix 4.*

Those who get involved in jail ministries are challenged to learn more, and are greatly blessed—not to mention they are storing up a few treasures in heaven.

*   *   *

What do you say to an AUTHOR?

It must be very exciting to have your stuff published and to know that it is having an influence in the world. My Father is an author. His books have been translated into more than 1200 languages, and they have been on the best-seller list for hundreds of years. Millions of lives (including mine) have been marvelously changed by reading His Words. Of course, I speak of the Holy Bible. Have you read it?

CHAPTER 11

In the Devil's Domain

*And the devil that deceived them was cast into the lake of
fire and brimstone, where the beast and the false prophet
are, and shall be tormented day and night forever ...*

REVELATION 20:10

A Witch in the Kitchen

Waiters and waitresses are usually too busy to stop and talk
while working, and the best thing you can usually do is just
to leave a tract on the table—with a generous tip tucked
inside. But this time it was different. It was too early in the
morning for most vacationers in Ocean City, so the
restaurant where my wife and I were having breakfast was
nearly empty. Our waitress looked very tired and depressed.
She had a sallow complexion, sunken cheeks, and bags
under her eyes.

When I asked "How ya doin?" She replied, "OK" and
then she surprised me by confessing: "Actually I'm very
tired and sleepy." Looking at her watch, she continued: "I
haven't had any sleep for about twenty hours."

"How come?"

"I'm working two jobs. I don't have time for sleeping."

That seemed like a good cue for me to say, "You better
pray that God will help you get some rest. You know—Jesus
said, "Come unto me and I..."

She cut me off. "Jesus was an idiot! He couldn't even
save himself. How can He save you? blah blah X blah X X
blah."

I won't repeat the rest of the garbage she spewed out.
But her bottom line was: "I am a Wiccan. I worship Satan."

I admit, I was not prepared for that, and she was out of
earshot before I could respond intelligently. I wish I had the

presence of mind to say, "I can see Satan is acting true to form. Just as the Bible says: he is the great deceiver and the destroyer—and he's already working you to death!"

That was my first sad experience with a practicing witch, but probably not the last. Have you looked in the religious section of a secular bookstore lately? The shelves are loaded with books about Satanic forms of worship; everything from Satan's bible to Edgar Cayce to Deepak Chopra, including hundreds of books about witches, ghosts, psychics, channeling, scientology, astral projection, astrology, candle-burning, aura reading, Wicca, Celtic Magic, The Isis Oracles, palmistry, and Tarot cards.

I ask myself—"why are people attracted to this garbage?"

I believe that every unredeemed person has a profound emptiness within the human spirit—like a vacuum that needs to be filled with something. And if people reject the Holy Spirit of God, unholy spirits from the powers of darkness will rush in to fill the void.

*　　*　　*

What do you say to a BUILDER?

That's a great profession. It's very satisfying to build something and then have something good to show for it. I used to work for a newspaper and it was kind of depressing to realize that my artwork would often be used to wrap the garbage in. But now I work for the greatest builder of all. I wonder if you know Him? He is building His kingdom in the hearts of men and it will last forever. His name is Jesus.

He was a murderer from the beginning...
And the father of lies.

JOHN 8:44

Demons Invade a Mental Hospital

In the summer of 1985, God opened a door for a group from our church to share the gospel once a week in a mental hospital in Maryland. Although this ministry bore much fruit in the long run, the particular adventure I'm going to relate to you now didn't. But I'll tell the story because it teaches a valuable lesson about dealing with demons.

As soon as we walked into the meeting room one night, a young man approached me and said: "Preacher—you gotta help me. I'm scared!" He was trembling all over and looked desperate. "I'm hearing voices. They tell me to kill myself. I'm really scared."

I asked one of the other guys in our group to take charge of the meeting while I led the disturbed man into a small room where we could meet privately. There was a mat on the floor. He fell on the mat, blubbering, trembling, and crying almost incoherently. After I shut the door, I knelt down on the floor beside him and tried to talk to him. He was shaking so much he could hardly talk. He just kept saying the voices were telling him to kill himself.

This was my first experience with this kind of thing, but according to what I had read and heard, I was convinced that he was possessed or oppressed by demons. When Jesus told his disciples in Mark 6:17, *These signs will accompany those who believe: They will cast out demons in my name...* I understood it literally, so I did the only thing I knew: I spoke to the demons, "In the name of the Lord Jesus Christ, I command you evil spirits to come out of him."

Immediately the man quieted down, stopped trembling and crying, and fell asleep.

I thought, "Praise the Lord! Thank you, Jesus!" I left him there sleeping peacefully, and I went back to the meeting room to share the gospel with the others. I felt very pleased with myself for knowing what to do.

But, I'm sorry to say, the story doesn't end there.

A week later, when we went back to the hospital, I didn't see the man, so I inquired of his whereabouts. Several people told me he had killed himself two days ago!

That is not a misprint. The man whom I thought was rid of the demons died five days after I prayed over him.. He killed himself! And a little bit of me died with him when I realized what had happened.

How did it happen? No one would discuss the details. What a kick in the head! Why? Why? Why? I kept asking myself and God. I believe I found the answer in Matthew 12:43-45: "Jesus said, *"When an evil spirit leaves a person, it goes into the desert seeking rest but finding none. Then it says 'I will return to the person I came from.' So it returns and finds its former home empty, swept, and clean. Then the spirit finds seven other spirits more evil than itself, and they all enter the person and live there. And so that person is worse off than before. That will be the experience of this evil generation."*

Now I realize what probably happened. I had read that scripture many times, but I did not understand how to apply it. That was the mistake I made. Yes, the Lord did cast out the demons when I prayed in the name of Jesus—but that was only part one of a two-part process that should take place.

Please, dear Reader, you must understand this, so that you will never make that same mistake!

This is what I should have done: I should have kept him awake long enough to make sure he understood the gospel, then help him pray to receive Jesus as his Lord and Savior. Then Satan could have no power over him. Again, as the Word says, 1 John 4:4, ...*because the Spirit who lives in you is greater than the spirit who lives in the world.*

Epilogue

Once in awhile, God encourages us by letting us see a little glimpse of the fruit that we had a part in cultivating. Recently, after leaving a tiring two-hour session at the detention center in Annapolis, I went to a McDonalds to get refreshed. As soon as I walked in the door, I heard someone holler, "Hey Warren!" He was a former mental patient I remembered from the days when we shared the gospel at Crownsville Mental Hospital.

It had been eight or ten years since I had seen him, and I often wondered what had happened to Chris. He seemed extremely glad to see me, and he was nearly bursting with excitement to tell me all about his church, and his involvement with evangelism. What a blessing to see him looking so good and growing in his walk with the Lord.

Then the very next week, after leaving the detention center, I went to a Borders Bookstore to check out the Christian Book section. I found a book that looked interesting and sat down in a lounge chair to read for a while. A young man seated next to me kept looking at me like he was studying my face. Finally, he said to me. "I know you. Your name is Warren Sears. You used to come to Crownsville and teach the Bible several years ago." What joy!

He thanked me for our ministry there and told me he was looking for a good church. Incidentally, I was able to give him a copy of a paper I had just written entitled "How to find a good church." Thank you, Lord Jesus.

*　　*　　*

For God hath not given us the spirit of fear;
but of power, and of love, and of a sound mind.

2 TIMOTHY 1:7

Dr. Jesus Wins ... at the Same Mental Hospital

A small group had been going to the Crownsville Mental Hospital on Friday nights for several weeks, holding typical gospel meetings in a big dayroom: singing hymns, reading scripture, telling stories, giving testimonies, preaching. But a certain patient named Rick would not stay in the room. He just sat on the floor in the hall within earshot, just outside the room. We often tried to talk to Rick, but he wouldn't say two words to anyone.

Our last visit to this hospital was a large blessing. As soon as we entered the room, Rick practically ran to greet us. This is exactly what he said: "Hey Warren, I got right with God, and I got my mind back!"

"Hallelujah! That's wonderful Rick," I said, "But what do you mean when you say—you got right with God?"

"Well, I heard you guys preach last week—and I finally realized that Jesus took the punishment for my sin when He was crucified. I thanked God that He has forgiven me, like the Word says, '...though your sins are as scarlet; they shall be as white as snow.' So I asked God to help me live from now on according to His will."

What a joy! I knew from other things he said that he was without a doubt a new creation in Christ. The guy that never talked was now bubbling over and spilling out words a-mile-a-minute. He couldn't wait to tell me the whole story, but I will give you the condensed version:

Several years ago, some of his drinking buddies brought him home one night drunk as a skunk. The next morning when he woke up he couldn't even remember how he got home. When he finally staggered downstairs with a huge hangover, he discovered his mother lying on the floor dead. He called the police and they arrested him as a possible suspect for murder. The autopsy showed that she died from a blow on the head, and later one of the guys that brought him home that night confessed to the murder.

Although the court cleared Rick from being an accomplice, he always blamed himself for his mother's death—and he had been plagued for years with feelings of guilt! He withdrew from everyone, and had even attempted suicide.

There's a perfect example of how Satan can hit someone with a triple whammy. First, Rick's religion had taught him that it's okay to drink in moderation. But there's a problem—when the alcohol begins to work, the difference between *moderation* and *excess* becomes blurred, and Rick got so drunk he couldn't find his way home.

Second, Rick hangs out with evil companions who kill his mother in a foiled robbery attempt.

Third, although he confesses he is partly guilty and asks God to forgive him, Rick cannot accept God's forgiveness. We should not be surprised at this because Satan is the great accuser. Revelation 12:10, "*... the accuser of our brethren is cast down, which accused him before God day and night.*" Satan constantly reminds us of our failures. As long as he can keep us in that defeated state of mind, we will never be a good testimony for the Lord.

Well, thank you, Jesus. After several weeks of sitting in the hall listening to the preaching, the marvelous light of God's Word finally penetrated Rick's darkened mind. With people like Rick, unredeemed psychiatrists and mind-dulling pills just don't have the ability to get to the root of the problem. But Dr. Jesus had the answers.

With thanks to the Gideons, we gave Rick a pocket-sized New Testament and urged him to read it daily, and to please, when released from the hospital, look for a good bible-believing, bible-teaching church, where he would be able to fellowship with strong Christians.

I'm reminded of Hebrews 4:12, "*For the word of God is living and powerful, and sharper than any two-edged sword, piercing even to the dividing asunder of soul and spirit...*

And is a discerner of the thoughts and intents of the heart."
I loved Rick's statement: "I got right with God—and I got my mind back!" Hallelujah!

*   *   *

***But I say unto you, that whosoever looketh
on a woman to lust after her hath committed
adultery with her already in his heart.***

MATTHEW 5:28

Adult Books… Or Kid Stuff?

It was a chilly, rainy, dismal night in November. Bob Cate, a friend of mine, and I, hoping for opportunities to witness to parents, went out to visit our third-grade Sunday School kids. We spent two hours sloshing from house to house, but no doors opened to us. Mothers would crack the door a couple inches and say things like, "I'm sorry. David's gone to bed. Could you come back another time?"

"Sure," I think to myself, "twelve-year-old boys always go to bed at seven-thirty. I should have known."

"Oh Lord," I prayed, "This is very frustrating. I'm all fired up to preach to someone tonight—but no one wants to listen. So what do I do now?"

Finally, about 8:30, we gave up on the Sunday School kids. I dropped off Bob at his home in Bowie, and started driving towards my home in Beltsville—all the time praying that I would see someone to preach to.

The rain was coming down hard now. Not a soul was on the street; no stores were open after nine o'clock; and there was not even a hitchhiker on Route 1. Wait a minute—I did see one store open. What kind of store? Oh no! It's an adult bookstore! Of course, they would be open. Doesn't the devil operate twenty-four hours a day?

Pulling over to the curb, I prayed, "Lord, do you really want me to go into this hell hole? You know how I hate these places."

He reminded me that Jesus said, "*I will build my church, and the gates of hell shall not prevail against it.*"

No doubt I had my marching orders, but I still resisted: "But Lord, suppose someone sees me going in there. Suppose someone recognizes me. They will get the wrong impression. I could lose my testimony."

However, God was not buying my excuses. He reminded me of the big black cowboy hat on the back seat which I had picked up when my wife and I were vacationing in Colorado. It made a good rain hat, and if I pulled it way down over my face, no one would recognize me.

"Okay Lord, just give me the words to say. I'm on my way."

Whoosh! I burst through the door like Marshall Dillon—and looking neither to the right nor to the left—I stomped straight back to the man behind the counter. Glaring at him from under the brim of the big black hat, and with as much disdain as I was capable of, I snarled, "Do you call this an adult bookstore? THIS IS KID STUFF! Do you want to see an adult book?"

Shoving my big black Bible under his nose, I thundered, "THIS is an adult book! It's God's Word, the Holy Bible. It tells all about God's love for you—and God's purpose for your life. God hates the filthy garbage you are selling in this dump."

He stared back at me with little beady eyes—dumbfounded and speechless.

I became aware of two or three customers slouching around in the shadows, so I talked loud enough for them to hear. "You are wasting your life working for the devil. You better get out of here before he destroys your soul. God created you for a higher purpose!"

I don't recall the rest, but I'm sure it was a very short message. I felt like the place was full of demons! Ugh! What a stinking place! I handed him a tract and got out of there.

*　　*　　*

What can you say to a TEACHER?

That's a wonderful profession. My friend is the greatest teacher that ever lived. Things He taught two thousand years ago changed the whole world, and they are still changing lives for everyone who believes in Him and gives God control of their lives. Of course—His name is Jesus!

For we wrestle not against flesh and blood,
but against principalities, against powers,
against the rulers of the darkness of this world,
against spiritual wickedness in high places.

EPHESIANS 6:12

Scripture Warns Fortune Tellers

Driving merrily along one summer morning, I passed a Fortune Teller's office in Cheverly, Maryland. Seeing that sign keyed in a memory of a time when the Lord miraculously delivered me from those types of satanic forces—and prepared me for this encounter.

I recalled a time when my niece, Patsy, was involved with a form of witchcraft. Her literary teacher at a state college in Salisbury, Maryland got her and another student interested. They read books on the subject and actually went to cemeteries to call up ghosts!

At first, they thought it was all just fun and games—something to entertain the kids with on Halloween. But when they actually experienced manifestations of this stuff, they were horrified. Tables moved across the room by some invisible force, and when they worked a Ouija board, the pointer virtually raced around the board. It was demonic—spelling out answers to questions with uncanny accuracy, and making frightening prophetic statements—all calculated to undermine our faith in God!

Anyway, when I, being a fairly young Christian, heard about those things, I went to a library to check out some books on the subject.

As I entered the reference section, the first book my eyes fell on was a Schofield Bible. That interested me because that very week, a very spiritual brother in my church had mentioned having a Schofield Bible. Being curious to see what was so special about it, I paused in my search for books on the occult to take a quick look. Flipping it open at random, I saw a big footnote at the bottom of the page.

"Ah," I thought, "so that's why the Schofield Bible is so special." The footnote said, briefly: *"Eight banned practices for determining future actions are those of diviners, astrologers, enchanters, witches, charmers, consulters of mediums, necromancers.* In other words, "Don't touch it."

Oh how I love Jesus! Once again, He had sent an angel to watch over me—the bible had opened to Deuteronomy, 18.

Naturally, I left the library without looking any further.

Now—years later—I made a U-turn and drove back to the fortuneteller's office. I felt a need to warn her; just the way the Lord had warned me. The "Madam" had not arrived yet, but a young lady who worked there was sitting on the steps waiting for her. I thank God she was still young enough to have an open mind. She gave me permission to sit beside her and share something from the Bible, so opening to Deuteronomy 18, I showed her the same passages that had rescued me from the occult. There was just time to share this along with the Gospel before the madam arrived.

As the madam approached, she looked irritated when she saw my Bible. She probably suspected that I was not there to have my fortune told. Anyhow, she said, "Good morning, can I help you?" There was ice in her voice.

"Actually, I was hoping that I could help you." I said. "I wonder if you know what the Bible says about this business that you practice. According to…"

She angrily interrupted, "You don't have to tell me what the Bible says! I advise you to mind your own damn business and get away from here before I call the police!"

Starting to walk away, I offered one parting comment, "It is my business to warn you! God loves you—but the business you practice is an abomination to Him. Yet He will forgive even that, if you are willing to let Him control your life."

She got in the last word, but it's not fit to print.

CHAPTER 12

Jesus Walks in the Parks

He has said, "I will never leave you nor forsake you."

HEBREWS 13:5

Singing Hymns to Demons

When I got off from work and began the long walk to the bus station at 12th and New York Avenue in the heart of D.C., it was about 11:00 pm and pitch dark. It had been a rough day and I was tired, so I decided to take a shortcut and walk diagonally through the park at 14th and K. After about ten steps into the park, I was suddenly aware this was not the safest place to be after dark. The air was putrid with the smell of alcohol, cigarettes, and unwashed bodies. It seemed like every wino and junkie in town was lurking in the shadows; just waiting to pounce on me. I fear that many people who use drugs are apt to become demon-possessed. "So what do I do now?" I silently prayed.

He reminded me, He lives in our praises... and demons hate to hear the name of Jesus. So I just walked fast straight ahead, and began singing at the top of my voice, "Praise the Lord. Praise the Lord. Let the earth hear His voice..." I was amazed at the way all the characters just scattered. I felt a little like Moses must have felt when God parted the Red Sea and all His chosen people walked through on dry land.

I guess this story is more about self-preservation than about witnessing. Anyway, every time I hear that song, I get a little excited as I'm reminded how God protected me that night.

*   *   *

For we cannot but speak the things
which we have seen and heard.

ACTS 4:20

A Sunny Day in May

This was an excellent day for planting seed. I sat on a bench near my office to eat lunch. A clean-cut looking man, probably in his early twenties, sat nearby reading a newspaper. As I ate lunch, I began to pray, "Lord, do you want me to speak to him? Then please Lord, fill me to overflowing with your Spirit. Give me a sign, and give me the words to say."

Suddenly the stranger put down his paper, turned towards me, and simply said, "Hi," clearly indicating he would welcome conversation.

So I replied, "Hi. I see you are interested in sports."

"Yeah. I was reading about the Orioles. Looks like they will have a great team this year."

Glancing at my watch, I knew I only had about fifteen minutes left of my lunch hour. If I was going to share the gospel, there was no time for small talk, so I quickly turned a corner, saying, "That's good. I like to hear about winners. If they don't win, I soon lose interest."

"Yeah, me too," he answered.

Then I say, "By the way, I have a friend that is no doubt the strongest man in the world. In fact, He is the strongest man that ever lived! I'd like to tell you about him." Now I really had his attention.

His eyes were saying, "Wow. Tell me."

"This man was whipped within an inch of His life; then He was hung up on a tree until He strangled; then stabbed in the side with a soldier's lance to make sure He was really dead. Then He was buried. But after three days, he walked out of the tomb, alive and well!"

I went on to explain the Gospel to him and answer his questions the best I could in the remaining ten minutes. Some

103

precious seed was planted. Walking back to the office, I prayed that God would send others to water the words that I had planted. And I trusted God to save him according to His perfect timing.

*　　*　　*

...forgetting those things which are behind, and reaching forth to those things which are before, I press toward the mark for the prize of the high calling of God in Christ Jesus.

PHILLIPIANS 3:13-14

A Rare Day in June

In the late nineties, I became acquainted with Drew Shofner, then the pastor of a nearby church, when he graciously gave me 15 minutes of pulpit time to demonstrate *Operation Salt and Light* (see chapter 16) to his congregation. The pastor was impressed. He asked where I attended church. I told him, and added that actually, I had been thinking about finding a church closer to home. Then he said, "Well, if you decide to come here, I would like you to be our Evangelism Director."

He was a dynamic preacher and encourager. The pianist, Janice Wood, played with a passion, the congregation was friendly, it was close to home, and the offer to be Evangelism Director was one I couldn't resist. So I began to attend there with my wife. However, we didn't join at that time because they had no provision for Helen to get around in her wheel chair.

A couple of months later, I gave the wheel chair away— because Helen was on standby for a brand new body and a beautiful mansion that Heaven's Number One Interior Decorator prepared for her.

Thank God for the Holy Comforter! He gives me that peace that passes all understanding—and He tells me to press

104

on…(Philippians 3:13-14) So I joined the church, with high hopes of becoming the Evangelism Director. But then, guess what! A couple of weeks later, the pastor announced he was being called to another church.

Well, meanwhile, I had made some good friends there, I became involved with the outreach ministry, they liked the sound of my saxophone, and I liked the new pastor, Mark Johnson, so I decided to stay on. A few months later, the main reason I initially started attending there occurred anyway—the new pastor asked me to be the Evangelism Director.

Now that the time had come, I wondered: "Am I really the man God wants for the job?" Suddenly, I wasn't sure. I felt that I needed to talk to the Lord about it. Therefore, I went to my favorite place to meet with Him—the park right next to my home.

This was a beautiful place and a perfect day to spend with the Lord. The sun was warm as it filtered through the trees. Birds were giving a spring concert as I strolled along the path that wound it's way through the woods and alongside a stream. God had planted a variety of little wild flowers next to the path just to express His love for us. It was one of those "zippydedooda days."

Now here comes the strange part: It seemed like I heard the Lord say, "So you think you are an evangelist? Okay, I want you to speak about Jesus to every person you come in contact with today."

I must confess, that seemed like a tough and slightly unreasonable assignment to me, but I've learned two things over the years since I began walking with God. First, when the Lord tells us to do something, no matter how strange it may seem, it's best to just say 'amen' and go do it. And second, He always enables us to do exactly what He says.

I spoke to many people that day about Jesus. But I can only recall a few contacts that are worth relating. And mostly, I only remember the opening remarks.

The first was a joy—a plain looking middle-aged woman walking slowly along the path in the opposite direction that I was going. She looked absorbed in her thoughts and not very happy. I simply said, "Pardon me, miss." She stopped walking and looked at me. "I believe God wants me to tell you something." I smiled and said, "You are very beautiful in God's eyes. He wants you to know that He created you in His image and He loves you very much!"

Her face lit up with a beautiful smile. She said, "Thank you. But how do you know God loves me?"

Because the Bible says, "God commended His love toward us, that while we were yet sinners, Christ died for us." (Romans 5:8)

That's all I recall of our conversation.

The next person I saw was a young lady pushing a baby in a stroller. Her eyes were red as if she had been crying. I just looked at her baby and said, "Aw, isn't she cute. Bless her little heart. I guess she's a girl 'cause of the pink blanket. What's her name?"

"Cynthia."

"Cynthia... Wow, a beautiful name for a beautiful child. God has truly blessed you, Miss."

She smiled and said "Thanks," but there was sadness in her voice. I felt awkward like I was intruding, so I made some ordinary departing remark and walked on. I soon came to an old familiar path off to the side and followed it to a little sandy beach—a secluded place where I often went for prayer.

Feeling like a miserable failure with my second encounter of the day, I fell on my knees in the sand and asked God to forgive me for trying to do His work in my own strength. I pleaded with Him to empower me with His Spirit for the work He called me to do—for I know that apart from Him we can do nothing (John 15:5). God heard my prayer and went with me back to the main path.

His timing was perfect. Cynthia's mother had gone to the end of the walk, turned around and was on her way back. I fell in step with her and let Jesus in me do the talking:

"Hello again. Please pardon me for intruding, but God has told me that you are very troubled about something. Jesus loves you very much—and He sent me here today to pray for you. Please tell me how I can pray for you."

The way she responded was amazing. She confessed with tears that she and her husband had been quarrelling, and she was afraid her marriage was falling apart. The Holy Spirit helped me pray for her—and to thank God for some of His wonderful promises to all those who trust and obey! She thanked me profusely for reviving her faith. Praise the Lord!

The next close encounter was with a young man named David who was standing on a bridge and tossing breadcrumbs to the ducks. We chatted a few minutes about ducks and stuff, and eventually, using the approach that evangelist Bill Fay teaches in his course on *"Sharing Jesus Without Fear,"* I asked him, "Do you have any kind of spiritual belief?"

He simply answered, "I'm Catholic. How about you?"

"I'm just a Bible-believing Christian. At the present time, I belong to a Baptist church, but I can worship at any church which teaches that the Bible is the Word of God. The most important thing for me is my personal relationship with the Lord Jesus."

"I really don't like to talk about religion."

"Me neither. Do you know Jesus hated religion?" I asked.

"What do you mean?" asked David.

"The religious Pharisees were His worst enemies. Remember how Jesus talked about them in the Sermon on the Mount? He said they liked to be seen standing on street corners making long prayers. They sounded a trumpet before them when they gave alms. Then in Matthew 23, Jesus really got rough on them. He said, *'Woe unto you, scribes and Pharisees, hypocrites!'* repeatedly. They thought that their good works gave them special favor with God... But the scripture says that in the eyes of God, *"...all our righteousness are as filthy rags."* (Isaiah 64:6)

I've learned one way to deal with most Catholics is to let them see how little they've learned about the Bible—especially regarding salvation, and the many precious promises God has given in His word. So I continued, "But, thank God, at least one of the Pharisees, Nicodemus, was open to the teaching of Jesus! Do you remember what Jesus told Nicodemus?"

"No, not off-hand."

"Well David, this is a saying that gets kicked around a lot these days, but I believe it's one of the most profound things that Jesus taught!" Taking a New Testament out of my pocket, I pointed to John 3:3. "Read this David. Jesus is talking to Nicodemus." *'Verily, verily, I say unto you, Except a man be born again, he cannot see the kingdom of God.'* I went on to explain what it meant to be born again and shared my testimony with him.

The bottom line: David said he would think about it.

The next person to come along was a pharmacist out walking his dog. He recognized me as a customer in his store, so we naturally exchanged a few pleasantries. His dog was beautiful. He obviously loved her very much, so she became the opener for conversation as we walked along together.

He felt like talking and he said, "You know, I've been in business now for about 15 years, and I'm sorry to say—I've come to the place where I can't trust people. So many times, people who I thought were good friends eventually disappointed me—when I learned how they would cheat, lie, and do anything to make a buck. So now, the best friend I have is this dog. She is always a true friend. I can depend on her. She's always so glad to see me. I can talk to her and know that she won't twist my words and betray my confidence. She would give her life for me."

Wow, what an open door to share the love of Christ. Praise the Lord! "Well Doc, I know how you feel. The bible says that people are basically selfish. In fact it says that *'All have sinned and fall short of the glory of God.'* It even says *'The heart is deceitful above all things and desperately wicked.'* (Jeremiah 17:9) But there is one whom you can trust with everything you have! He wants to be your friend—so much so that He gave His life for you... Nearly 2000 years ago at Calvary...etc., etc."

Doc listened to the whole gospel that day.

One other encounter that day that I recall was with a lady at the bank. She had to go with me into a little room while I took my wife's jewelry out of a safety deposit box. This gave me the perfect opportunity to share with her that my wife no longer needed these little baubles because she had put her faith in the Lord Jesus, and where she was now she was walking on streets of pure gold.

What a glorious day the Lord gave me!

*   *   *

Redeem the time for the days are evil.

EPHESIANS 5:16

This Adventure Almost Cost Me a Dollar

I had to work late on this particular night, so about 6 o'clock I went out for supper and a short walk in the park before returning to the office. Two men were at a picnic table drinking beer, and although it was beginning to get dark, I felt a strong impression that the Lord wanted me to witness to them.

Realizing they may feel uneasy about a stranger approaching them in the dark—when I was still some distance from them, I held up a dollar bill and called out, "Hello. I'll give one of you guys a dollar if you let me talk to you for five minutes."

The younger guy laughed and said, "OK. Give me your dollar and go ahead and start talking." He looked at his watch, and said "But I can't guarantee you that I'll listen."

He listened a few minutes and then he confessed, "I used to be a Christian, but I drifted away from the Lord and haven't even been to church in years. But I know what you say is true, and I'm making a decision right now to start going back to church again. I appreciate you talking to me. And please—take your dollar back."

No problem. Hallelujah!

* * *

CHAPTER 13

All in the Family

*The natural man receives not the things of the Spirit of
God for they are foolishness unto him...*

1 CORINTHIANS 2:14

An Eighty-Year-Old Babe in Christ

This man was a mystery to me. Although he occasionally
attended a local church to please his wife, his ears were deaf
to the gospel. He had just enough college—Darwinism and
all that malarkey—to undermine his faith. He said he could
not believe in anything supernatural. He only believed that
Jesus was a great moral teacher, but no more than that!

Yet, in spite of this, he had lived a remarkably good life.
He taught his children to live by the 'golden rule' and as far
as I know, that's how he lived. Anyone would be glad to
have him for a next-door neighbor.

With a wife and five kids, he had to struggle to keep
food on the table during the depression years. He began a
career of teaching public school and was soon promoted to
the position of principal, but still didn't earn enough money
to make ends meet. So he quit the teaching profession and
worked as a Fuller Brush salesman for a few months.

Then in 1929, the year of the big crash on Wall Street,
the family moved to Washington, DC and he went to work
serving a milk route for Thompson's Dairy. That was a
tough job! He had to get up at midnight, catch a bus to the
dairy, load up the truck with milk and eggs, drive through
residential areas, hop off and on the truck and carry milk in
glass bottles in all kinds of weather—rain, sleet or snow. In
the summertime, he'd get home at 1or 2 in the afternoon—
sometimes later if he had to collect bills at the end of the
month—and then work a half acre vegetable garden. That

was the routine for about ten years until he got promoted to sales manager for the company.

When I became born again, I often tried to persuade him to believe in Jesus, but we always ended up in arguments. He loved to argue; and he stubbornly clung to his belief that all so-called miracles could be explained by natural phenomena.

To make things worse, he occasionally attended a church that was nothing more than a social club. So I tried taking him to other churches. I thought if he could just experience a church where there was real fire and excitement, it would make a difference. His reaction: "Those people must think God is deaf!"

Finally, I realized that it was a waste of time to argue with him, but I never stopped praying for him.

One time when we talked, God gave me an idea: Although it seemed quite unorthodox to me—not the usual way to share the gospel—I really felt it was from the Lord. This is what I said: "I've been thinking." (That caught his attention.) "I know you say that you don't believe in the deity of Christ, or anything supernatural. Yet it seems to me that you live more like a Christian than many Christians do. You're honest. You're generous to a fault. You made many sacrifices to support your family during tough times. The only time I ever heard you cuss was when you dropped a big hunk of ice on your foot. And that wasn't so bad. You just made reference to the son-of-a-female dog. I don't understand how you could live such a good life without the power of God in your life. I know you were brought up in a Christian home. I knew your older sisters—they were all Christians. I bet when you were just a little kid, your sisters took you to Sunday School and you sang *Jesus Loves Me*, and Jesus came into your heart...and He has been there ever since! But you don't know it."

I know that sounds goofy, but for once, he didn't argue. He didn't say anything. He just sat there quietly for quite awhile, probably recapturing some good childhood memories. We never brought the subject up again.

The next week he went back to Tennessee, where he had

lived with his daughter, Faye, ever since his wife died. Not long after that, I heard he responded to an altar call at her church and was baptized. How I thank God for the testimony of Faye and her husband, Dr. Tom Campbell.

I know his conversion was real, because the next time he came to visit, he sat and read Christian books with tears streaming down his face. These were the same books that before, after reading a couple pages, he tossed aside.

What a blessing to see the glorious change in this eighty years old man! Although the change was not necessarily enormous, because it appeared that he really had lived a good life. The most visible change was seeing that peace which passes all understanding—as he began "Leaning on the Everlasting Arms."

He had the joy of his salvation for six more years before the Lord called him home. He enjoyed helping to construct a new building for my sister's church, and I heard that during his last stay at the hospital, he kept the nurses laughing—told them he would like to marry one of them, but they were all so wonderful he couldn't decide who to bless.

There's a lot more I could say about him, because—just in case you haven't guessed—he was my Dad! HALLELUJAH!

*   *   *

What do you say to a PLUMBER?

I know the greatest plumber that ever lived. He put a pump in my chest that if it is properly maintained it could work for 100 years or more. Then He installed several miles of pipes carrying blood and oxygen to every part of my body. And when all that wears out, He'll give me a new life in Heaven. Jesus can do the same for you, if you give Him control...

For He shall give His angels charge over thee, to keep thee in all thy ways. They shall bear thee up in their hands, lest thou dash a foot against a stone.

PSALM 91:11-12

An Angel Got Into the Act

Like most of the women on my wife's side of the family, our niece, Audrey, was truly beautiful. Every place she went, men turned their heads for a second look.

But when Audrey was only 18 years old, cancer took her mother's life, and her father had to work two jobs to pay all the medical bills, so she and her younger brother and sister came to live with us for a while. Helen, my wife, loved them like she would her own children, and she was very concerned that in Audrey's confused state of mind, she would fall for the first guy who made a play for her.

Naturally, Audrey and her siblings were mad at God for taking their mother—so all of our attempts to counsel them with spiritual things only seemed to aggravate them. In fact, they would get angry if we tried to 'preach' to them.

So the only way we could get across anything spiritual or interject God into any conversation was when we said 'grace' before the evening meal. I always tried to say it differently in order to catch their attention. One night I felt inspired to pray, "Lord, we thank you for this wonderful meal; thanks for providing all of our needs. And God, we especially thank you for giving us angels to watch over us and protect us from harm."

The next day when Audrey came home from work, she was all excited. She said, "Uncle Warren! Something really weird happened today on my way to work." (Audrey worked at the old courthouse in Upper Marlboro, Maryland. To reach her office, which was below ground level, she had to walk down a long flight of steep concrete stairs.) "When I started down those back stairs, I tripped and lost my balance. I started to fall headfirst. I thought for sure that I was gonna

bust my head wide open. But suddenly, someone grabbed
my arm and held me up 'til I could grab the rail. I looked
around to thank whoever it was. But there was nobody
there!"

"Wow! Remember last night at the dinner table," I said,
"we thanked the Lord for giving us angels to protect us."
God planted some powerful seed that time! Audrey's faith
got a jump-start. To this day (about 20 years later), she and
her devoted husband are raising two fine boys and faithfully
serving the Lord in their local church.

*　　　*　　　*

So then faith cometh by hearing,
and hearing by the Word of God.

ROMANS 10:17

If Any of You Lacks Wisdom...

Are you worried about a child or a grandchild who has not yet received the Lord? If so, this story will probably bless you very well.

As I was walking from a hospital to the adjacent parking lot one day, I heard an old man call out in a singsong voice, "Has anybody got time for Jesus?"

He was sitting on a park bench about fifty feet away. Naturally, I was intrigued, and delighted to meet another Jesus freak, so I called back, "Yes, I have time for Jesus." I walked across the lawn, sat down next to him, and Elder Roscoe M. Brown and I just chatted for a while like we'd known each other for a hundred years. He was as wise as he looked with wooly white hair and mahogany complexion. Then he told me this remarkable story:

"I had been concerned for a long time that one of my grandsons, Jeremiah, was fifteen years old and still was not saved. So one day I said to him, "Jeremiah, your old granddaddy's eyesight is failing, and I fear that some day I won't be able to read my Bible. You're a good reader and you have a good voice. I wonder if I could hire you to read some of the Bible aloud—and record it for me on your tape recorder. Then, when I can't see to read any more, I can listen to the tapes. I'll buy the blank tapes and I'll pay you by the hour—more than you can earn working at McDonald's or someplace."

Jeremiah was eager to earn some extra money, so he started to work right away. First, I had him read the book of Ecclesiastes, and then he started on the gospel of John. After completing the sixth chapter of John, he came down to breakfast one morning and announced to Granny and me, "I have decided to give my life to the Lord."

116

Oh what wisdom the Lord can give to his children—as He said in James 1:5, *"If any of you lack wisdom, let him ask of God!"*

*   *   *

What do you say to a BOOKEEPER?

What a coincidence! I was just reading about an incredible Bookkeeper that keeps records of every person that ever lived. The book is called The Lamb's Book of Life. Everyone who has received Jesus as their Lord and Savior has their name in it—and they are guaranteed a place in Heaven. Do you know whether your name is there?

But if the Spirit of Him that raised up Jesus
from the dead dwell in you, He that raised up Christ from
the dead shall also quicken your mortal bodies by His Spirit
that dwells in you.

ROMANS 8:11

A Doubting Thomas Sees the Light

My father-in-law, Thomas Garretson used to run into the woods behind his house and hide when he saw me coming. (That's what my wife told me.)

His unhappy childhood filled him with bitterness and distrust for religion. He was "farmed out every summer," as he said, to live with an uncle who professed to be a Christian. He made him work hard in the fields all day—no time to play, no fun, and no love! They just used him for cheap labor. Then, to top it off, as he said, "On Sunday, we spent half the day settin' in church. I couldn't play ball or anything cause I had to stay dressed up—and sit around on somebody's porch all afternoon listening to the old folks talk, and then go back to church again that night!" He hated religion! But he survived his unhappy childhood, married a sweet country girl, and had five beautiful daughters and one fine son.

Tom was in his forties, and I was 18 when we became acquainted where we worked at the Navy Yard in Washington, DC. He offered me a job playing sax and clarinet in his dance band on weekends. I soon persuaded the other sax player in the band, Helen, which was his oldest beautiful daughter, to become my wife—with his blessing.

Because of our mutual love for music, Tom and I became good friends. We always enjoyed each other's company, until that remarkable day when I became born again—and didn't know when to shut up from talking about Jesus. (New Christians often just can't understand why everyone doesn't see the light. Thank God for His Word that lets us understand those who are lost. I Corinthians 2:14 says *"The man without the Spirit does not accept the things that come from the Spirit of God, for they are foolishness to him, and he can not understand them, because they are spiritually discerned."*)

For the next forty-some years, I learned when to shut my mouth and when to overlook Tom's cussing and occasional temper tantrums. In fact, I learned one of the most effective ways to witness to anyone is to look for opportunities to help them.

One Saturday when my wife and I went to visit him at his home, Tom was hard at work renovating a room. I determined not to say one word about Jesus—not even a "praise the Lord." Instead I just picked up a scraper and paintbrush and went to work right beside him all day. That evening at mealtime, he shocked everybody by asking me to say the blessing.

Eventually, he became one of the best friends I ever had! We had a lot of fun together: going fishing, playing jazz—he played guitar and bass fiddle—pitching horseshoes, shooting pool, and helping each other in many practical ways. Everything was cool as long as I didn't talk too much about Jesus. Helen and I just kept praying for him—and praying that in time, he would see a little bit of Jesus in us.

Now Tom and Virgie (Helen's mother) started slowing down when they were in their eighties and—so that Helen could take care of her mom during a time of recuperation from a stroke—we all lived together temporarily in our one-bedroom apartment. They used our bedroom, and we slept on a sofa bed in the living room.

Other than saying grace at meals, we still kept "Jesus talk" to a minimum. However, one morning, just before leaving to go to work, I prayed that God would give me something to say to Tom. The Lord put a thought in my head, so I simply said, "Tom, I want you to do me a favor today. Please just think about this: God said, 'Let there be light.'"

His expression said, *Warren is weird,* however he nodded "okay." He had mellowed quite a bit in his old age.

That evening after dinner, Tom sat on the sofa looking at a tabloid newspaper Helen had left lying around, and when I sat down next to him, he said, "Have you ever heard about this Shroud of Turin?"

I thought, "Wow! So this is what the Lord had in mind when he told me to ask Tom to think about God saying, 'Let there be light'" I said, "Oh sure. I saw a film about it recently."

"So what is it?" He asked.

I told him the story briefly: "This cloth was found in the tomb where Jesus had been buried. They believed it was Jesus' burial cloth. And it has an image that looked like Jesus. No one could understand how the image was made, so recently scientists have been making tests to figure out what caused the image. Skeptics thought some artist painted it, but the tests didn't show any trace of paint or dye. Most observers agree it looks like a photographic image had somehow been transferred to the cloth by an extremely bright light!"

So, if Jesus was buried in a tomb," Tom asked, "where did the light come from?"

"Do you remember the news story about the U.S. testing an atom bomb in some desert out West? Well, after the test, they found a cloth that had been left lying on a rock about ten miles away from the bombsite. An image of the rock was found on the cloth that looked similar to the kind of image that was on the Shroud of Turin. I guess when Jesus had laid in that tomb for three days, God just spoke—like in the beginning of the world, when He spoke, 'Let there be Light,' and there was light! But think about it: that was no small thing. When God said, 'Let there be light', the sun, moon and stars appeared. I believe it's connected to that."

"What do you mean?" asked Tom, "How can that be connected?"

"There's a connection between God's power and God's light. Jesus said, "I am the light of the world.""

"Hell. I never did understand that. I just don't get it."

"Well, Jesus had been dead for three days. Only God could have the power to raise Him from the dead. I believe that somehow God's mighty power filled that tomb with a light nearly equal to the atom bomb explosion! The neat thing is the Bible says, 'If the Spirit of Him that raised Jesus from the dead dwells in you, He that raised up Christ from the dead shall also give life to your mortal bodies.'"

"Where is that in the Bible?" Tom asked.

I opened my Bible and let him read it for himself. It was Romans 8:11, which is one of my favorite verses that I memorized.

About two hours later, after we had all gone to bed, Virgie called me to come into the bedroom. Tom was shivering and trembling. Virgie said, "Tom wants to say that prayer with you."

I said, "What prayer?"

Tom said, "You know—the prayer you say to be saved."

By the way, after praying to receive Jesus, he stopped shivering and trembling and went to sleep.

Soon after that, Tom and Virgie moved back to their

own house and Tom enjoyed about a year of his new life in Christ.

O, THANK YOU, LORD JESUS. HALLELUJAH!

NOTE: There is a lot of controversy about the authenticity of the shroud. I don't know whether it is authentic or not—I just thank the Lord He used it to on that occasion to make Tom see the Light!

*　　*　　*

What can you say to a FARMER?

My Father was a fantastic farmer. He not only made everything grow that is good to eat—but He designed the seeds, produced the soil, and caused it to be watered every morning. He even planted a tree that had twelve different kinds of fruit on it. He called it the Tree of Life, and He said if you eat of it you would live forever. Do you know what happened? He wrote a Book called the Holy Bible that tells all about it. I know it's true.

CHAPTER 14

"Unshackled!"

*And He said unto them, "Go ye into all the world
and preach the Gospel to every creature"*

MARK 16:15

Aired on 1,473 Radio Stations Worldwide

How would you like to have a dramatization of your story broadcast to millions of people around the world? This is a unique opportunity for many Christians to be a witness to multitudes of people.

The program is called "Unshackled." It's a 30-minute old-fashioned radio drama produced by the Pacific Garden Mission in Chicago. The dramas are based on true stories and listeners have submitted most of them. I had listened to this program on local Christian radio stations for many years, and I particularly appreciated the stories because they high-lighted events that lead up to someone's conversion, and they always made the gospel very clear. Some of the stories are also printed in little booklets that make great tools for witnessing.

They often encouraged Christians to submit their stories, so after retiring from full-time employment in 1988, I learned to use a word processor, and sent them my story. They called it "From Jazz to Jesus." It was all about my deliverance from obsessions for fame and fortune, when I gave control of my life to Jesus.

It was a great pleasure to work with them. They asked me to write the story much longer than necessary and allow them cut it down to fit the 30-minute format. Mainly, to make it more interesting, they changed some of the narrative parts into dialogue, but the facts stayed the same. When the editor phoned to tell me they planned to use it, she requested that I send them a tape of my voice so they could choose an actor whose voice was similar to mine. I thought they did a great job of matching my wife's voice.

They also invited me to come to Chicago and be there when they taped the show. I was not able to attend at the time; however, it was lots of fun and very exciting to listen to the broadcast.

It was translated into Spanish, Arabic, Romanian, Russian, and Polish for broadcast around the world. They sent me a booklet listing the times and call letters of every station in the U.S. that aired it. Several of my siblings and relatives in different parts of the country heard it on their radios. They also sent me a recording that I could give copies to unsaved friends and relatives.

Let me encourage you to submit your story. It's great fun! They will gladly send you all the guidelines. The address is: Pacific Garden Mission, 646 South State St, Chicago, IL 60605.

*   *   *

What do you say to a COMPUTER PROGRAMMER?

Would you like to meet the greatest computer programmer that ever lived? And I don't mean Bill Gates or Al Gore. I'm talking about the one who designed an absolutely amazing computer that only weighs 3 or 4 pounds and everybody has one hooked to the top of their neck! The designer's name is Jesus Christ. He came to earth 2000 years ago just to pay for our sins...and restore our relationship with the Heavenly Father. I believe everything the Bible says about Him is absolutely true. He waits to meet you with open arms.

CHAPTER 15

The Warren Musiclight

*...mystery of God, and of the Father, and of Christ,
in whom are hidden all the treasures and knowledge.*

COLOSSIANS 2:2-3

Music for the Hearing Impaired

One night the Holy Spirit ministered to me in a very unusual
way. I woke up at about 3:00 am, wide awake from a sound
sleep and—for no special reason that I knew of—a mood
came over me to silently thank the Lord for so many
wonderful blessings: just simple things—like my wife asleep
beside me; our son, Steve; our good health; our friends in the
church; on and on it went. A strange warmth flowed through
me—unlike anything I had ever experienced before, and I
sensed that God was very close to me. Also, I had an
expectation that God was going to show me something...

As I continued lying there, quietly praising God, I began
to see lights flashing on and off on the bedroom wall. Many
colors of the rainbow were turning off and on in a controlled
rhythmical pattern. Although there was no accompanying
sound, I had the feeling I was looking at music!

I looked out the window to see if I could discover the
source—perhaps someone fooling around with flashlights
and crystals. But I saw nothing. I could only conclude that
God produced it in some mysterious way. The vision only
lasted a couple of minutes, however, it was very vivid.

Was God showing me a kind of visible music that could
be enjoyed by deaf people? I remembered when I had played
my sax at a Christmas party recently and a deaf man put his
hand on the bell of my horn just to feel the vibrations. At the
time, I thought, "How sad! That's the only enjoyment deaf
people experience from music!" That had been pressing on

my mind lately, so perhaps God was answering an unspoken prayer. Still wide-awake, I got up and found an art book with an illustration of a spectrum color-wheel. Excitedly, I counted the colors. Just as I thought: there were _twelve_ different pure colors in the spectrum. Wow! There are also _twelve_ different musical tones in the chromatic scale in one octave. Yes! It made sense.

On that same day, I saw a teenage neighbor of mine, Maurine Carney, who had deaf parents. She was the first

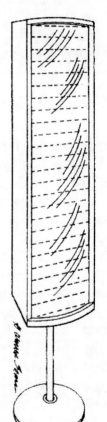

person, other than my wife, with whom I shared the vision. When I described an instrument featuring 24 spectrum-colored lights that could be activated by a piano keyboard, Maurine thought her parents would love it and encouraged me to pursue it.

I became so excited! I talked about it with nearly everyone I saw— using it as a conversation opener to talk about Jesus.

I felt that God had given me an awesome responsibility to use this concept of visible music to minister the wonderful works of God to the deaf community. But I had not learned to wait on the Lord. As a result of this vision, I guess I was on a perpetual emotional high and had become caught up in a whirlwind of activity— which left very little time to spend with my precious wife. That was my first mistake.

I persuaded Harry Cook, a dear cousin who is mechanically skilled, to build the first model, with a silent piano keyboard (two octaves) for demonstration, and within a few months my deaf neighbors borrowed the model of the **Warren Musiclight** for a Christmas party. They all took turns playing it, and those who had lost hearing due to illness still remembered songs from their childhood. They could recognize tunes from rhythmic patterns and the rise and fall of melody lines. It was especially effective for jazz and classical tunes that had very distinctive melody lines. Maurine told me they had a lot of fun with it!

In order to meet more deaf people, and also learn to communicate with sign language, I quit my regular job and took a job at the Washington Post newspaper, where they employed hundreds of deaf printers. The Post let us use a room for Bible studies every morning before work—which gave me many opportunities to share my testimony as I personally invited nearly every one in the composing room to attend. Julius Goldberg, a Messianic Jew, interpreted for the deaf.

Next, I showed the Musiclight to the chaplain and students at Gallaudet University—a school for the deaf. They all enjoyed it and used it in several programs, including a rock concert in the auditorium. It lent itself well to the song, *This Little Light of Mine*. One of the teachers at Gallaudet liked it so much she wanted to order ten of them to use for teaching. But, sorry to say, I was not able to produce them in time, or for a reasonable price.

Several months and $1,000 later, Harry and I designed and built a prototype of a portable piano keyboard attachment that will adjust to fit any piano, which allows hearing people as well as deaf people to enjoy it!

I was greatly blessed by several godly men all along the way who encouraged me—including a patent attorney, Tom Moran, who helped me write a patent application (granted in 1976), and Bob Young, who helped me improve the design for the keyboard attachment.

Leo Paulin, a creative promoter and successful business man, saw the model where it was being used at Adelphi Bible Church a few times. He told me he could sell one to every bar on Connecticut Avenue—a busy street that runs for miles through Washington, DC and Bethesda, Maryland—which is probably the address for at least twenty nightclubs. But because I believed God gave me the vision, I felt sure God wanted it to be used only for worship, I rejected his offer—another mistake! Hindsight shows me that the man who invented the piano probably did not worry about trying to control where it could be played!

Riverdale Baptist Church in Largo, Maryland let me test it in an adult Sunday School class for deaf worshippers. It was a great disappointment for me when after two Sundays, I learned it was not suitable for worship—because the important elements in hymns are the words—not the melody. So when they sang about 'green pastures' while red and yellow lights were flashing; or they sang 'washed by the blood' while green lights were flashing, it was very confusing to the congregation.

It is great when the colors precisely fit the lyrics— which rarely happens—and I am concerned that we should never obscure the meaning of inspired worship music for the sake of abstract artistic values.

Suffice it to say, I made many more mistakes after that concerning this invention. Life became too busy—working around the clock; learning to speak sign language; running to and fro to all kinds of meetings to drum up support for manufacturing; making video film presentations, etc.

Probably the worst mistake I made that almost wrecked our marriage was not trusting Helen's gift of discernment— as I nearly formed a partnership with a man whom I thought was a spiritual giant, but later discovered he was not trustworthy—just as Helen predicted. As I listened to the counsel of ungodly men, I became mentally exhausted, and ready to give it all back to God.

I gave the original model to Chaplain Rudy Gawlik at Gallaudet and decided to move on with my life—and focus on my main calling to be a fisher of men.

To conclude, I praise the Lord when I recall the delight I saw in the expressions of many deaf people that saw it, so I still believe the vision came from God. I was told that a movie called *Mr. Holland's Opus* had something very similar in it. Perhaps there was some connection.

Business Opportunity for the Reader

For someone with business acumen, there is a wide potential to profit from the manufacture and sale of the Warren Musiclight. As demonstrated, many hearing-impaired people naturally enjoy abstract musical elements such as those found in jazz and classical music—where lyrics are not important—and with the high-tech capabilities that exist today, my original design for the piano keyboard attachment could be greatly simplified, mass-produced and marketed for an affordable price.

I will be happy to show my model and share all my notes, construction plans, and promotional ideas with anyone who is seriously interested in pursuing it.

Contact me at gwarrensears@aol.com.

*   *   *

What Do You Say to a PRINTER?

Printing is a wonderful profession. I'm so thankful for a great printer named Johannes Gutenberg. First he invented movable type, then he invented the Gutenberg press. Until then, very few people had the opportunity to read the Bible. There was a monumental change in the course of human history, when the Gutenberg Bible made it possible for thousands of people to learn about Jesus. Do you know Him?

CHAPTER 16

Operation Salt and Light

Ye are the salt of the earth: but if the salt have lost his savor, wherewith shall it be salted? Ye are the light of the world. A city that is set on a hill cannot be bid.

MATTHEW 5:13a -14a

Gospel Posters... Powerful Attention Getters

God planted seeds in my mind for a ministry called *Operation Salt & Light,* when He gave me the following experience:

Two or three saints from our church used to share the gospel every Friday night at a mental hospital in Crownsville, Maryland. Usually fifteen to twenty adults, suffering from all kinds of mental illnesses, were in the room where we ministered. We held typical gospel meetings—singing, testimonies, preaching and praying—and tried to get everyone to participate to some degree.

At that time, the nurse on duty was a Christian, and she let us hang a poster of a Bible verse on the wall, which we would refer to when one of us preached. When the meeting was over, we just left the poster there and brought another one the following week. Usually, during the interim, the poster would disappear, but one Friday there were four of our posters there—one on each wall.

That evening, everybody but one middle-aged woman, participated. She appeared to be extremely disturbed. She paid no attention to anything that was going on. She just walked around and around the room the whole evening, carrying on a conversation with some invisible being.

A week later, as soon as we entered the room, that same woman quickly walked over to me. She looked so peaceful and composed; I didn't recognize her until she told me the following story:

"Preacher, when I came here last week, I was so upset...so confused... I didn't know who I was or where I was. I couldn't stop walking around this room, and after awhile I began reading these signs you all put up. I looked over there and I read, *"God so loved the world* ...(she quoted John 3:16). Then I looked over there and I read, *"Jesus said, I am the way, the truth, and the Life..."* On and on she went and she quoted all four signs. She continued, "I just kept going from sign to sign. After awhile I had them all memorized, but I just kept going around reading them over and over again! Preacher, I can't tell you what a wonderful effect they had on me. They made me realize the important things in my life... and get things in the right perspective."

Well, praise the Lord! Of course, we prayed with her. We never saw her there again.

This experience dramatized the incredible power of God's printed Word, and planted seeds in my mind for the ministry I named OPERATION SALT AND LIGHT.

Soon after that, while walking at lunchtime, and praying for a guy who was as lost as a blind goose flying backwards in a hail storm, I noticed a row of trees that had just been planted equal distances apart. Suddenly, in my mind's eye, I saw Christians standing where the trees had been—quietly holding up cube-shaped signs with gospel verses.

Was this vision from God? It seemed like a practical way to communicate the gospel—an easy way for all Christians to be witnesses—to impact people who might otherwise never be exposed to God's Word. But I kept questioning: Would God really use signs? He reminded me of the disturbed lady in the mental hospital. He reminded me of the sign that He Himself carved on a rock up on Mt. Sinai. He reminded me that His Word is *"...quick and powerful and sharper than any two-edged sword, piercing even to the dividing asunder of the soul and spirit, and of the joints and marrow, and is a discerner of the thoughts and intents of the heart.* (Hebrews 4:12). Was God actually calling me to get this thing going?

At first, like Jonah, I wanted to hop a boat to Tarshish and forget about it. But I sure didn't want to be swallowed up by a big fish. God kept giving me confirmation every time I prayed about it. I shared the vision with my pastor and other mature brothers. I felt quite sure that some spiritual leaders in my church would grab the idea and run with it. But that didn't happen. Although many thought it was a good idea, that's as far as it went.

I believe God was teaching me a lesson: when He gives someone a vision to serve Him, He is usually calling them to make it happen. He reminded me that I was a graphic artist. He arranged all my circumstances; He forced me into early retirement; gave me the place to work; money to get started; Christians to encourage me; and just as I was about to give it up, the Lord burned another verse into my mind: Isaiah 59:19, *"When the enemy shall come in like a flood, the Spirit of the Lord will raise up a standard against him."*

That did it. I said, "Amen, Lord"… and that was the birth of the ministry that went public with the Word of God.—OPERATION SALT AND LIGHT, in the summer of 1995.

Calling All Christians

"When the enemy comes in like a flood, the Spirit of the Lord will lift up a standard against him." Isaiah 59:19

. . .to go public with the Word of God!

OPERATION SALT & LIGHT offers a practical way for the whole body of Christ to share the glorious Gospel of Jesus to a skeptical, lost and dying world.

Hundreds of God's people, prayerfully . . . and joyfully holding up powerful Bible verses, which can be read from 30 to 50 feet away, dynamically displayed on two-color four-sided posters . . . highly visible in public places, wherever crowds of people are present.

We will not march. (It is difficult to talk to someone that is marching.)

We will not protest. Isn't it better to light candles than to curse the darkness?

We will not condemn anyone. Christ came not to condemn, but to seek and save those who are lost!

We will simply stand quietly in prayer, as we hold up God's Word . . . and be ready to testify of Him when opportunity is given!

LET US CLAIM GOD'S PROMISE IN ISAIAH 55:11
"My word that goes forth out of my mouth shall not return unto me void, but it shall accomplish that which I please . . . "

This is a copy of the first page of my brochure (reduced to 53% of the original size) that I use to promote the ministry.

The first four signs were hand-lettered with markers and mounted with duct tape on discarded egg boxes. Old broom sticks inserted through the middle and tacked to one end served as handles. Although crude, they served as models to demonstrate the concept to my church. Many brothers said encouraging words to me after the demo.

My vision enlarged. I began to calculate the number of signs needed to stretch east and west along Pennsylvania Avenue all across Washington, D.C. Was this idea from God? Someone said, "It sure didn't come from Satan!"

Bob Young, a dear brother in the Lord, came up with a unique design for the cube-shaped cardboard frame with a PVC pipe handle. It folded flat for storage with the handle removed. The signs (sixteen verses) are each 12-inch by 12-inch by 18-inch, red and black on a white background, and laminated and mounted on the frame with silver-gray duct tape. The total weight of each sign: 2 1/2 lbs.

I thank God for Fred Booker, a Christian printer—operates as Victory Press—who gave me a ridiculously low price for printing the first hundred signs. And, my dear wife, Helen, emptied her savings account to help pay for the first round of printing, laminating, cardboard and PVC pipe!

My experience in graphic arts and speaking for the Gideons had prepared me well for most aspects of operating this ministry. I enjoyed designing the signs and promotional literature, and assembling the signs in my basement shop. I especially enjoyed speaking in churches where I was often allowed to give my testimony and present the gospel, as well as share the vision of *Operation Sat & Light* (OSAL).

Each year, eight to ten ministry events were planned, in Washington, DC and nearby. Some favorite ministry sites were college campuses; in front of museums; July 4th events in the parks; Annapolis Harbor; North Beach on Bayfest Day; festivals; any place where there were crowds of people. An average of four or five saints participated for two or three hours at each event. At least 5000 or more tracts were distributed. It was a special blessing for me when my 14-year-old grandson, Frankie, came along and passed out tracts. Many seeds were planted, and some precious souls were saved—only God knows how many.

The first ministry event was on Constitution Avenue at the well-known Annual Cherry Blossom Parade in Washington, DC. Ten brothers with eight signs lined the sidewalk. One man walked along reading all the signs and when he got to me at the end of the row, he said, "Man! I feel like I just walked through the Judgment Hall." He kept on walking before I could respond.

In Annapolis, two of us were holding an OSAL sign on Main Street when four teen-age boys approached. They looked very troubled about something. One of them asked us, "Do you believe in evolution?"

"Of course not! That's false science straight from the pits of hell!," I responded. (They had hit on a subject that I hate with a holy passion.) "God created you in His image—and He has a wonderful purpose for your life. Why do you ask?"

They told me they went to a Catholic school and they understood that the Pope had said that it was okay to believe in evolution. I remembered reading about that in the newspaper so I was not shocked.

I said, "Let me ask you a question. Do you believe in the Lord Jesus?"

They all said yes. So I picked a Bible story that probably every Christian schoolboy is familiar with.

"Do you remember when Jesus was in the wilderness fasting and praying for forty days and Satan tried to tempt Him? Satan said, *If you are God, command that these stones be made bread. And Jesus answered, It is written, Man shall not live by bread alone, but by every word that proceeds out of the mouth of God."* (Matthew 4:3-4) So obviously, Jesus believed in the account of creation according to Genesis. So who are you going to believe? Jesus, or the Pope? One of them didn't know what he was talking about!"

They saw the light, so we went on and shared the Good News, just in case they were ready to give their lives to God.

There were many wonderful opportunities the Lord gave

us to witness for Jesus through OSAL but one more needs telling:

The campus at University of Maryland had always been a favorite place of mine to go witnessing. Campus Drive was a public street and we understood that according to the first amendment of the Constitution we could legally go any where on that street. And we went there for two years in a row with no problem. But then in 2002, our last time there, things changed!

On the day before we were scheduled to go there with the ministry of OSAL, I helped the Gideons do their annual Bible distribution there. In the past, they had always had unlimited access, but this year the university officials made restrictions—and the Gideons were only permitted to be at one small designated area near the Student Union Building. As a result, only 3,000 New Testaments were given away—compared to 10,000 in the year previous—one more instance where Christians are losing the freedoms our forefathers fought so hard to gain!

Upon learning that the same restriction would apply to OSAL, I became disheartened and began phoning our members that evening to tell them our ministry at U. of M. was cancelled. The last person I called—a dear brother named Fred Brennan—said, "That's a violation of our rights. I'm going to go!"

I thought about Patrick Henry. I knew Fred was right, and it was no use to try to dissuade him. So I said, "Okay. If you go, I'll go with you."

Fred and I stood about twenty feet apart on Campus Drive. We were not in the official designated area. I had an OSAL sign and a stack of gospel tracts. Fred had a strong desire to see the salvation of Jews, so he stood with a huge Israeli flag, and passed out tracts proclaiming Jesus as the Messiah. Fred's beautiful flag with the big Star of David attracted much attention. Eight or ten Jewish students crowded around talking to Fred, and discussions became pretty lively.

Everything went well for about twenty minutes, until a campus guard arrived on the scene and politely told us about the new ordinance—and I politely told him about the first amendment to the Constitution—as I kept on giving out gospel tracts, even as we spoke.

About ten minutes later, a squad car parked at the curb with a county policeman and an official from the university. They politely read the new ordinance to us and offered to give us permission to move to the designated area.

Fred (always very respectful) answered, "I believe this is a violation of our right to free speech. After a little more discussion, Fred politely said, "I'm sorry, but if you insist on making me move, you will just have to arrest me."

Again, the college official tried to persuade us to recant, but the policeman indicated he would be quite willing to arrest us if necessary. At that point, I spoke up and politely told the policeman, "I'm sorry Sir, but I don't have time to be arrested today. I have a three o'clock appointment in Annapolis."

Then I told Fred, "Fred, if you insist on being arrested, you're on your own. May God be with you."

Fred was kept behind bars at the jail in Hyattsville until 10 o'clock that evening waiting to see a judge. The charge was *trespassing*... and his trial was set for two weeks later. But, praise the Lord, Fred was rejoicing because he had an opportunity to witness for Jesus to four guys in the cell with him. (Now is that the heart of an evangelist, or what?)

Fred had fasted and prayed for three days before the trial, and God really gave him wisdom to defend himself. Fred found a similar case from 1983 on the Internet, and offered it to the judge as a precedent for his defense.

I believe the Lord totally confused the prosecuting attorney. When she gave her closing statement, she kept repeating the same thing over and over like a broken record. (Incidentally, after the trial was over, we walked her to her car, and shared the gospel with her.)

Hopefully, we can use the trial transcript to persuade the University of Maryland to drop the restrictions next year.

By the way—the verdict: *Not Guilty!*

THANK YOU, JESUS.

Space doesn't permit reporting all the divine appointments that God set up through OSAL. Perhaps, if God wills, that will be the subject of another book.

Meanwhile, I took a sabbatical in order to seek God's wisdom to make the ministry more effective; to take time to know God better; and to write this book.

Properties of Salt:
Salt cleanses, purifies, and kills the poison of Satan's lies.
Salt melts the icy indifference that many people have to God and His church today.
Salt adds flavor to ordinary aspects of life on earth.

Properties of Light:
Light drives out the darkness of fear and death.
Light exposes the hidden sins of the unredeemed.
Light illumines the path of God's children.

Help Wanted

I'm praying that God will raise up more brothers and sisters to be leaders in *Operation Sat & Light* and help to expand the ministry wherever God leads.

If God is calling you to this ministry in your neck of the woods, I will do everything I can to help you get started. You may visit my shop in Bowie, Md. and I will show you step by step all phases of the work, including manufacturing, administration details, presenting to churches, and arranging ministry events.

Contact G. Warren Sears, 12707 Beaverdale Lane, Bowie, MD, 20715. Toll-free Phone (888) 779-4280.
Gwarrensears@aol.com

CHAPTER 17

Letters to the Editor

*And the Word of the Lord was published
throughout all the region.*

ACTS 13:49

The *Bowie Blade-News* Published This

One more example of a powerful way Christians can be a
witness is by writing *letters to the editor* that tie in with
current events. This can affect many people who may not be
reached any other way.

The following letter was sent to five newspapers in
Washington, DC and Annapolis shortly after the shooting of
students in Columbine High School in Colorado in March
2001. Maybe more papers would have published it, if it had
been shorter. I pray that more Christians will let their views
be known on this subject—via this avenue.

I thank God for the *Bowie Blade-News* for publishing
this. The only change they made was in the heading. My
original said: **Why are kids killing kids?** (I liked that better.
I supposed they changed it because it was too long to fit the
column width.) Here's what they ran:

Coping with violence

Sir:

The pundits say the solution is: Eliminate the violence that is
portrayed in TV, music lyrics, and video games; and to
exercise more gun control and more parental supervision. All
of this sounds reasonable, however a basic underlying factor
is largely being overlooked today:

Charles Darwin was a brilliant man in his day (1809-1882) and his Theory of Evolution was widely accepted by many of the scientists of that age. But that was 150 years ago. Today, with the vast increase of knowledge in all science disciplines, his theory has lost all credibility. In fact, many studies prove that it is not only false teaching, but it has a tremendously damaging influence on the way mankind views itself.

It's high time to remove this antiquated teaching from public schools. Of course, it won't be a quick fix, because a large part of four generations have already been deceived by it. Adolph Hitler loved it. It gave him the excuse to kill millions of Jews. Likewise Stalin's genocide. And then there was Madalyn Murray O'Hair.

For those of you who still follow Darwin, consider what he wrote in *Origin of the Species, 1859:* "To suppose that the eye with all it's inimitable contrivances for adjusting the focus to different distances, for admitting different amounts of light, and for the correction of special and chromatic aberration, could have been formed by natural selections, seems, I freely confess, absurd in the highest degree."

Near the end of his life, Darwin said: "I was a young man with unformed ideas. I threw out queries, suggestions, wondering all the time over everything, and to my astonishment, the ideas took like wildfire. People made a religion out of them."

Darwin realized his mistake! But it was too late—his books were selling. And like Frankenstein's monster, they took on a life of their own. Like the monster, not much good comes from it. Kids get the message: we are accidents of nature, without purpose, without meaning, without divine guidance, and without any moral absolutes. We have no spirit, and no soul, therefore we become obsessed with our bodies, obsessed with pleasure. Philosopher Ravi Zacharias put it like this: "there is nothing in history to match the dire ends to which humanity can be led by following a political and social philosophy that consciously and absolutely excludes God."

Scientists who have made major contributions to the world—Louis Pasteur, Isaac Newton, Michael Faraday, George W. Carver, to name a few, understood that wherever there is design, there must be an intelligent designer.

I'm not saying that we should teach religion in public schools, but at least we should stop undermining the biblical faith of our founders who made our country a great and powerful nation. When people have faith that God created us in His image, that He loves us, and He has a wonderful purpose for our lives, as the Bible teaches—this establishes a solid foundation for us to respect and appreciate life.

G. WARREN SEARS, Bowie, MD

Author's Note:
See Appendix 3 for suggested reading on this subject.

*　　*　　*

What do you say to a FISHERMAN?

I'm very glad to meet you, my friend. Have you heard about the man who had been fishing all night and caught nothing? Then in the morning, a man standing on the shore told him to go out again and cast the net on the right side of the boat. He did that—and one hundred and fifty-three great fish swam into his net. That was just one of the miracles Jesus did to demonstrate the incredible power and love of God. Do you know Him? He would like to be your friend.

Part Two: Helps

CHAPTER 18

Testimonies

And they overcame him by the blood of the Lamb,
and by the word of their testimony...

REVELATION 12:11

Your Testimony is Like None Other

God can use your testimony to reach someone for Christ who may not be reached by anyone else. And what joy—because every time you tell someone about your conversion experience, you will recall the miracle of being born again—and how wonderful it felt to know that all your sins were forgiven! Christ gave you His cloak of righteousness, and now you can stand unashamed in the presence of a holy God.

It's a good idea to write it out and practice telling it in three to five minutes. But be flexible—vary the details to identify with whomever you're talking. Keep in mind—the purpose of your testimony is to make the unbeliever hungry and thirsty to know the Lord the way you do. Therefore, minimize the negative, put on your happy face, and emphasize the positive.

When time allows, here's the best way: First of all, pray silently that Jesus will give you a supernatural love for this person. Ask questions to get him (or her) to talk about himself—his job; his hobbies; his family; his goals. Demonstrate genuine interest in the person by listening intently. Look for areas in his life where you have mutual interests. In other words, establish some rapport, tell a funny

143

story, relax, and feel comfortable together. Then when the time seems right, you begin your story something like this:

PART I: "I'd like to tell you about an experience I had when I was __ years old that made a remarkable change in my life."

Now you tell about what your life was like before you gave control to Jesus. Try to share something from your past that will help your listener identify with you. Be brief, but offer enough details to make it real.

PART 2. Describe the circumstances and your frame of mind that led up to your conversion experience. Most non-Christians think that salvation comes through doing good works, so you need to make it very clear that there was nothing you did to earn your salvation. You do not want to come across as being *self-righteous*—as Christians are often accused of being. In fact, you can say that according to God's standards of behavior, you should have been stoned to death. But praise God, He is merciful.

Here's the place to briefly share the whole gospel: including the birth, death and resurrection of Jesus on the third day; He's preparing a place for us in heaven; and He could come back at any time to snatch us up to Glory.

PART 3. Concentrate mainly on these points: How did your life change after you were saved? Were you set free from any bad habits? Do you now have peace of mind no matter what the circumstances? Do you have more confidence? Have you found a purpose for living? How does God give you strength to get through the hard places? How does the Holy Spirit comfort you in times of tragedy? Do you ever feel joyful for no apparent reason? What about Psalm 37:4 in your life? - *"Delight yourself in the Lord and He will give you the desires of your heart."* Is it true? And what about Romans 8:28. Is it true?

PART 4. Assure the person that "what God did for a sinner like me, He can do the same for you." Ask permission to show them the Bible, and then take them down Romans road. Lead them in prayer. Give them a brotherly hug; a good tract, a Bible, tell him to read the Gospel of John ten times. If possible, take them to church next Sunday and watch them get baptized. And shout "Hallelujah!" at the top of your voice.

3-Minute Testimony Example

About 2000 years ago the Son of God was born in Bethlehem. That was the miracle of Christmas and God's gift to the world.

But for me personally, the greatest miracle happened in 1951. I was 28 years old and about as skeptical as they come. There was a time when I enjoyed reading about Jesus, but sorry to say, I had put Him in the same category with Superman, Tarzan, and Santa Claus. I just did not have the faith to believe that anyone so wonderful could really exist.

Well, so what? I was doing pretty good, at least I thought. I had a good job, a new car, a beautiful wife, a bouncing baby boy and even enjoyed playing in a jazz band on weekends. According to this world's standards, I should have been deliriously happy, but guess what—no matter how much I accomplished or how much I attained in this world, I had an emptiness inside that nothing satisfied. Sometimes I was just plain miserable. Why? I didn't know it then, but sin had separated me from the love and friendship of God.

Praise be to God, in a moment of despair, a Christian acquaintance spoke to me about God. Her faith was contagious. She reminded me of the 23rd Psalm that I had learned as a kid in Sunday School. Those words came back to me with a supernatural power. And for the first time in six years, I prayed to God.

I still recall my exact words—I said "God, if you are real, I want to put my life in your hands. I want you to take control of my life." That's when my miracle happened. In the Gospel of John, Jesus calls it being born again. The third stanza of "O Little Town of Bethlehem" says it very well: ..."*No ear may hear His coming, But in this world of sin, Where meek souls will receive Him, still the dear Christ enters in.*"

I'd love to tell you all the wonderful things God has done in my life since the Spirit of Christ came into my heart, but that would take too long. But for now, just let me say He has given me a new heart—that loves that which He loves and hates that which He hates. His perfect love casts out all fear. He comforts me in times of sorrow. He gives my life purpose and direction, and gives me the pleasure of serving Him in His Church. He gives me joy and contentment just to be a member of His family and enjoy the fellowship of men and women in the church who love Him. The greatest thing is—I know that my sins have been forgiven, and Jesus is preparing a place for me in heaven! I will love Him, enjoy Him, and praise Him forever.

5-minute Testimony Example

When I was 28 yrs old, I had an incredible experience that changed my life. Until then, I thought I was doing pretty good. I had a beautiful wife, a cute little baby boy, a good job, and a new brick bungalow in the suburbs. I even played in a jazz band a couple nights a week.

I should have been very happy, but I was never satisfied. I always wanted more. I was anxious about many things. I had a lot of stomach aches, and I was hooked on cigarettes. I started to acquire a taste for booze, and fantasize about women. My friends were either atheists or hypocritical Christians. I felt like I couldn't trust anyone and I didn't like the guy I had to look at in the mirror when I shaved every morning.

I reached an emotional crisis when I felt that my boss was going to steal an idea from me. I impulsively decided to go to his house on a Saturday night and have a showdown with him. He took time to reason with me and I realized I had been mistaken—and then he suggested that I talk to his wife.

She was the kind of person who radiated with love and joy. Like some of the lovely ladies in my church, her faith was contagious. So I talked to her about some things that had been worrying me. She said we needed to 'rise above' those things. She mentioned that God is love. Then she told me that when Charlie (her husband) got upset, she read him something from the Bible. She asked me if I knew the 23rd Psalm. Yes. I recalled it as a kid in Sunday school.

On my way home that night, I began to think about the 23rd Psalm, and I thought—that is so beautiful, perhaps it really is the Word of God, like these Christians say it is. Well, I pulled my car off the road, and I simply prayed: "God—if you are real, I want to put my life in your hands. Please take control of my life." Then I went home to bed.

The next morning, it was like seeing the world for the first time. I had a strange feeling that God was with me—and I had that peace that passes all understanding that Jesus talked about. I never saw the sky so blue and the grass so green. I fell in love with my wife in a deeper way than I had ever experienced before. She thought I had cracked up. She kept saying, "What's happened to you? You don't seem like the same person. You've always been so self-centered. Now you notice everything that's going on. I thought you didn't believe in God. But now, you say God is here with us. I don't get it."

Now comes one of the greatest things that happened to me—just like Jesus said would happen in John 16:7-11: Jesus said "...*the Holy Spirit will come and reprove the world of sin, righteousness and judgment to come.*" That very afternoon I began to get flashbacks of all the mean, rotten, selfish things I had done in my life, going all the way back to childhood. I fell on the bed in a heap—crying a river. Thank God my wife understood the gospel and told me how when Jesus was crucified He paid for my sins—and I am forgiven.

A few days later, I met a Christian who spoke about being <u>born again</u>, and I realized that's what happened to me. When I asked the Lord to take control of my life, the Holy Spirit came into my human spirit and gave me the power and desire to live a life that is pleasing to God. That is the greatest miracle that God is doing on the earth today! As it says in II Corinthians 5:17, *"If any man is in Christ, old things are passed away. Behold, all things become new."*

When God created the first man and woman on earth, they walked and talked with God. That was normal. But when they disobeyed God, they tried to hide from God—which is impossible. Sin separates us from God. That's why Jesus said, (John 3:3) *"Except you are born again, you cannot see the kingdom of heaven."*

It's all about having a personal relationship with God. We must believe that Jesus died to pay the penalty for our sins, and accept his gift of salvation. There is no other way to fully enjoy His presence now and in eternity. As Jesus said, *"I am the way, the truth, and the life. No one comes to the Father except through me."* (John 14:6) Please ... read the Gospel of John with prayer that God will reveal the truth. Then commit your life to Him... and ask Him to lead you to a good Bible-believing, Bible-teaching church.

*　　*　　*

What do you say to a LANDSCAPE ARTIST?

That is a wonderful profession. It must give you great joy to help make the world a more beautiful place to live in. By the way, did you see the beautiful sunrise this morning? My Father designed that just to give us a little hint of how beautiful heaven is going to be. Incidentally, do you know for sure that you will go to heaven when you die?

CHAPTER 19

Gospel Tracts

My Word that goes forth out of my mouth shall not return unto me void, but it shall accomplish that which I please.

ISAIAH 55:11

Don't Underestimate the Power of Tracts

A witness for Jesus should never leave home without a few good tracts in his pocket. Would a carpenter go on the job without a hammer and saw? Or would a fisherman go to the river without any bait?

A tract is especially useful when you begin to share the gospel with someone, but time runs out before you can tell the whole story. Or, suppose you are able to share the whole story, but they are not ready to make a decision. If you give him or her a good tract, it will reinforce and confirm the things you have taught. (My son was saved when he read a tract, *Four Spiritual Laws,* three days after it was given to him by a couple of guys who shared the gospel with him.)

Many excellent tracts are available in Christian bookstores, and you can learn a lot about sharing the gospel just by studying them. But select with care. Some do not make it crystal clear that a person must be willing to give God control of their life. If you use these, there is some danger that the readers may only receive Christ as their Savior, and not accept Him as Lord of their life. Therefore, many call themselves Christians who think that since Jesus died to pay for their sins, it's okay for them to keep on living in sin, and their lives look no different than those who still walk in darkness.

Personally, I like to write my own tracts—then I know that I can back it up with scripture. Following is one I wrote for general purposes and I've given out thousands. This fits on both sides of an 81/2 x 11 paper. You are free to copy any part of it, or all of it, and use it as a witnessing tool.

What are you looking for?

Purpose for Living * Love * Excitement
Friendship * Peace * Joy * Freedom
Success * Contentment * Forgiveness
Strength * Confidence * Hope

All of the above… and so much more… can be yours, when you simply agree with God and give Him control of your life.

First, consider these PROMISES one at a time in the light of God's Word (the Bible). Then I'll tell you how it can all happen for you.

PURPOSE FOR LIVING God created you in His own image.[1] You are unique and He has planned a special and wonderful purpose for your life[2] that only you can fulfill.

LOVE God is love.[3] When He comes to live in your heart, you will experience a new intense love for God and others that you have never known before. God's perfect love drives out all fear.[4]

EXCITEMENT When you say "YES" to God and receive His Son, Jesus Christ, as your Lord and Savior, it is exciting to sense the presence of the Almighty God in your life… and to discover the wonderful life He has in store for you as He leads you day by day![5]

FRIENDSHIP You will become part of the family of God along with all the dear people of the world who have given their heart to Jesus. Just think of it: The creator of the universe will become the best friend you ever had.

150

PEACE Even when turmoil rages all around you, "... the peace of God, which passes all understanding shall keep your hearts and minds through Christ Jesus."[7]

JOY Jesus speaks of His joy being in us and our joy being complete.[8] And He mentions nine different blessings in the Sermon on the Mount. Peter referred to "joy unspeakable." That's why Christians sing and shout their praises to God.

FREEDOM It's great to be free from addictions; free from worry; and free from guilt and shame. "The law of the Spirit of life in Christ Jesus has made me free from the law of sin and death."[9]

SUCCESS "Delight yourself in the Lord and He will give you the desires of your heart."[10] The Lord gives you a new life with new desires.[11]

CONTENTMENT Jesus said, "Seek ye first the kingdom of God and all these things shall be added unto you."[12] King David wrote, "A little that a righteous man has is better than the riches of many wicked."[13]

FORGIVENESS "If we confess our sins to God, God is faithful to forgive us our sins and cleanse us from all unrighteousness."[14]

STRENGTH "They that wait upon the Lord shall renew their strength..."[15]

SELF-CONFIDENCE "If God is for us, who can be against us?"[16] "He that began a good work in us shall perform it until the day of Jesus Christ."[17]

HOPE "Christ in you, the hope of glory."[18] Hope for today, tomorrow, and hope for eternity.

*All of the above are standard benefits for the normal **born-again** Christian.*

Notice the phrase *born-again* is emphasized. It comes from the Lord Jesus (Gospel of John 3:3) when He said, "Verily, verily I say unto thee, except a man be born again, He cannot see the kingdom of God." He continued by saying we "... must be born of the Spirit."

Our human spirit is the organ God gave us to be filled with His Holy Spirit. Our human spirit has been damaged by sin—ever since Adam and Eve disobeyed God. Therefore, unless we have the infilling of God's Holy Spirit (sometimes called the Spirit of Christ) it is impossible to live a sinless life that is pleasing to God.[19] (See Romans, chapter 8)

It doesn't matter who you are. You may be a college professor, the governor of Maryland, or a drunken fool who is just one drink away from skid row... The Bible says, "all have sinned and fall short of the Glory of God."[20] The glory of God is Jesus, and no one can live up to His standard. That is why Jesus said, "You must be born again!" Only this can give us power to live according to God's Word.

We must choose between the Kingdom of God... and the Kingdom of Satan. Jesus gave us many warnings that there is no neutral ground; your choice also determines where you will spend eternity: either in heaven or in hell... there's nothing in between.

Therefore, the question is: How can YOU become born again? You can have that experience right now... if, as Jesus said, you will humble yourself as a little child... trust that God's Word is true... and talk to God in prayer! First of all, simply confess (agree with God) that you are a sinner and you are <u>willing</u> to repent (or turn away) from your sins. (Sin means disobeying God.) Thank God that He loved you so much that He sent Jesus to earth to teach us how to live. After His 33-year life on earth, He was crucified, died and buried, and rose again on that first Easter morning three days later. And thank God that Jesus' death on Calvary's cross paid the full penalty for the sins of all who believe in Him.[21] That is the Gospel (Good News)... and thank God, if you lack <u>the faith</u> to believe it, God will give you that also *just for the asking.* And finally, <u>ask Him to come into your heart and lead and direct your life day by day.</u>

It is all a gift from God! You can't earn it. No one deserves it. That's why it's called *"Amazing Grace."* Jesus Christ is the good shepherd... "He leads you in paths of righteousness for His name's sake."[22] In contrast to that, <u>all false religions</u> teach that you can earn your salvation by doing good works. The Bible declares, <u>"It is the gift of God: not of works,</u> lest any man should boast."[23] Jesus said, "I am the way, the truth, and the life. No one can come to the Father but by me."[24] I pray you will <u>surrender your life</u> to Jesus as your Lord and Savior today! It's very risky to put it off... because we are not promised tomorrow! God loves you, and so do I.

When you become born again, spiritually speaking, you are a baby, and you must begin to eat regularly from God's Word in order to grow strong in your faith and enjoy the reality of all that God has planned for you.[25] A good place to start reading is the Gospel of John in the New Testament. Read it carefully many times.

<u>Make haste to find a Bible-teaching church</u> to help you become better acquainted with Jesus, our wonderful Savior and Lord! (Sorry to say, these days many churches distort the teachings of the Bible... so pray that God will lead you to the right church.) Call me if you wish at (888) 779-4280. <u>I would love to hear from you</u>.

Warren Sears,
Director of Operation Salt And Light

Bible References: 1/ Genesis 1:26 2/ Romans 8:28 3/ I John 4:8 4/ I John 4:18 5/ Romans 8:14 6/ John 1:12 7/ Philippians 4:7 8/ John 15:11 9/ Romans 8:2 10/ Psalm 37:4 11/ II Corinthians 5:17 12/ Matthew 6:33 13/ Psalm 37:16 14/ I John 1:9 15/ Isaiah 14:31 16/ Romans 8:31 17/ Philippians 1:6 18/ Colossians 1:22 19/ Romans 8:8 20/ Romans 3:23 21/ John 3:16 22/ Psalm 22:3 23/ Ephesians 2:8 24/ John 14:6 25/ Matthew 4:4

The following is a one-page tract that I wrote to call attention to our Bible Study that was being held at Prince George's Community College.

GOD IS STILL DOING
MIRACLES!

2,004 years ago, God came to earth in the form of the man: Jesus Christ. He walked on water, calmed the stormy sea, turned water into wine, and commanded dead people to come alive, just to demonstrate His _POWER!_ He healed the sick, restored sight to the blind, and hearing to the deaf, just to demonstrate His _LOVE!_ Finally, He allowed himself to be crucified to pay the penalty for our sins, to demonstrate His _GRACE_... and to make it possible for you and I to enjoy the greatest MIRACLE of all!

Jesus Christ arose from the grave and opened Heaven's gates for all who trust Him as their Lord! Jesus loves you with an everlasting love. He has a wonderful plan for your life—for *NOW* and for *ETERNITY*. Are you willing to turn away from sin, and give God control of your life? Tell Him so in prayer, and ask God to fill your heart with His Holy Spirit and *give you the MIRACLE of NEW LIFE!*

You are invited to attend Bible Studies with the
CAMPUS BIBLE FELLOWSHIP
Monday and Thursday—12 noon to 1:00 pm

Author's Note: You are welcome to use this if you wish by substituting your own specific information re time and place.

154

Part Three: Final Answers

...so that I might finish my course with joy, and the ministry, which I have received of the Lord Jesus.

ACTS 20:24

My Final Answer to Satan

I wish I could print this on the bottom of my shoe where you, Mr. Devil, could easily see it. You should know that I am aware of your subtle strategies to stop the gospel from spreading. I know how you operate—your stupid lies, your temptations, your accusations, and your deceptions—and I'm here to expose you.

The following cartoon shows the forbidden fruit that you offer to all those people today who choose a hopeless and horrible death—by eating from the tree of knowledge of good and evil—rather than eating from the tree of life.

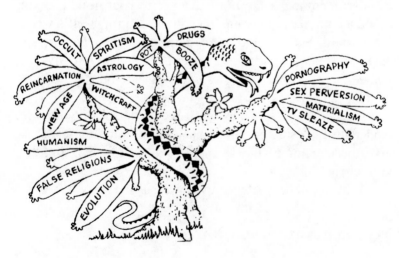

Your first strategy to stop the gospel is to try to convince new Christians that they do not have the "Spiritual

Gift of Evangelism." Nice try—but we don't need it, because we are all called to be witnesses, and our heavenly Father has empowered us with the Holy Spirit to do just that.

Another one of your strategies is to constantly remind us of our failures to "save" somebody. No dice—that's not our job. (But—oh, what joy—just to be there when the Holy Spirit saves someone. How you must hate it!)

Or you will try the other extreme: tell us what a great job we're doing and get us all puffed up. No thanks! We know what the sin of pride did for you. And we know that only the Holy Spirit has the power to save anyone.

By the way, I'd like to remind you that only one-third of the angels left heaven with you to be cast in the lake of fire and brimstone "...and *shall be tormented day and night forever and ever."* (Rev. 20:10). That means two-thirds of the angels are on our side.

My Final Answer to Druggies

When you pop a pill or smoke marijuana, you alter your normal state of mind. You open the file of that beautiful wonderful computer the Lord attached to your neck, and you invite the murderer to come in and take control. That's where Satan starts his evil program of misery. Then he just sits back and laughs while you get 'high' and slowly kill yourself. The Bible calls it sorcery (Deuteronomy 18) and God hates it.

One pill can give the 'destroyer' control of your life. And faith in Jesus, no larger than a tiny mustard seed, can give the Creator of the Universe control of your life! It's your choice.

Why not choose life—and give Jesus the final answer?

My Final Answer to Cults

You all have a few things in common. If your religion claims to be Bible-based, you distort the teaching, or rewrite the

Bible, or both! Also some cults base foundational beliefs on a person's teachings other than the Bible. And I thank God that many former members of your false religions have written books that fully expose your false prophets. (See Appendix 5)

All religions except Christianity teach that you can go to heaven if your good works outweigh your sins. May I ask you a question? How many good works must you do to earn your way to heaven? Isn't that a little scary? Suppose you lose count?

My Final Answer to Mental Patients

And I don't mean just the ones who are in institutions. Many mentally and emotionally disturbed people (not all—some have body chemistry problems) basically suffer from three things that psychiatrists are powerless to cure: GUILT, SHAME, and DEPRESSION. Praise the Lord—Jesus is the answer for all of that!

My Final Answers to Me

As I work on this book and review my experiences, I keep asking myself the question: what are the main things that I've learned about being a witness for the Lord Jesus—and have I succeeded in sharing them in these pages? No doubt, my experiences have taught me a lot, but I'm not sure this book puts enough emphasis on the main things. So, please forgive me if some of this is redundant. I will try to be brief in…

My Semi-final Answer to You

I know that according to John 15, apart from Jesus, we can do nothing. But if His Words abide in you, and you abide in Him, you can bear much fruit and give glory to God.

You must pray without ceasing—pray for boldness, pray for wisdom, and pray for the love of Christ to flow through you. Until people experience the matchless love of the Savior, they will probably never understand anything else.

If you are a clean vessel and filled with the Holy Spirit, He will give you the words to say and tell you when to stop talking. Your joy and peace should make unbelievers hungry to know God the way you do.

I attempted to show by these stories that Jesus does it all: He sets up divine appointments with those whom He wants us to witness. If you walk in the light as He is in the light, you will recognize His appointments and be ready.

When witnessing, you should always try to remember the example Jesus gave us—how he met people at the point of their needs—showing compassion and praying for them.

He came, not to condemn, but to seek and save those who are lost. Two witnesses are better than one—but remember, the one who said *I will never leave you or forsake you,* is always with you.

For more motivation to witness, learn these scriptures: 2 Chronicles 16:9, Romans 12:1-2; 1 Peter 2:9; Daniel 12:2-3; and Jeremiah 33:3.

As in most all things, you will learn by doing.

My Final Answer to You

THANK YOU! THANK YOU! THANK YOU!
The mere fact that you are reading this book tells me that you are one of God's special persons that I would surely enjoy meeting. It would be a terrific thrill to hear from you. And perhaps we would have a chance to get together for some extended fellowship.

If this book has helped you, you can multiply the work by passing it on to others in your church. If your local Christian bookstore doesn't have it, ask them to order it for you. Ask me questions if something is not clear. At the very least, tell me your name so I can pray for you. My phone number is (888) 779-4280. Email: Gwarrensears@aol.com.

My final answer: God loves you and so do I.

Appendices

Appendix 1.

A paper that I give to smokers that want to kick the habit. Printed originally on both sides of one sheet of 8 ½" x 11" paper.

LINCOLN FREED THE SLAVES
But what about you?

Are you chained to an addiction? Are you captive to a way of life that steals your pleasure? Here's good news!

If you really want to break free, and enjoy life more now and forever, this is for you! And it will not cost you a cent!

I'M NOT SELLING ANYTHING! NO PILLS; NO LECTURES; NO PATCHES; NO DOCTORS; NO CLINICS; NO CLUBS TO JOIN.

Maybe you're thinking: *"So what's your angle?"* It's simply this: I personally struggled for many years without success to overcome a habit that made my life miserable, and then one wonderful day I shall never forget... I was reading a great book and <u>two little words</u> stuck in my mind like a bright light that will never go out! And now, it is a great pleasure for me to share this with everyone possible! I just don't want anyone to suffer needlessly the way I did as I tried to quit an addiction for six years without success.

For me, the most obvious habit that enslaved me was

smoking cigarettes—but the principle holds true for any kind of addiction. At age 16, I thought it was pretty cool and I actually enjoyed it, but within a few years I grew to hate it! The cost; the smell; the dependency—like craving a smoke at 1:00 am—no butts in the ash trays; all the stores are closed and I have to get dressed and drive 6 miles to find a vending machine; and finally, that little cough won't go away ; and I begin to wonder if I'm getting cancer. So for the next six years I tried every cure on the market. Nothing worked.

Sometimes I'd quit for a day or two, and then suffered from such intense headaches that I slipped right back into it. Once while ruining our family vacation by becoming so grouchy, I actually quit for ten days. But then, it's back to work—a little bit of stress—and back on the weed!

Then comes the worst part: the terrible shame, the embarrassment of admitting to my friends that I lack the willpower to quit, and the awful loss of self-confidence! Not to mention the foolish waste of money. I was truly a slave far beyond the help of my medical doctor, and even Mr. Lincoln. And at last I gave up the idea of ever trying to quit again!

Now for those 'two little words' that broke the chains of my enslavement: I was reading the New Testament: Romans chapter eight, and in the first sentence Paul used the expression "in Christ." Those two words sort of popped out at me and I was very troubled to realize that although I considered myself a Christian, I did not understand what that meant. So, I began to pray:

"Dear God, I don't understand the meaning of "in Christ". I realize that Paul had a very close relationship with you—and you gave him knowledge of spiritual things that are beyond my comprehension. Dear God, I would love to know you the way that Paul knew you."

In my mind, I heard the voice of God answer very distinctly, *"Clean up your act"*. This is not quite the style of speaking that we would expect from God, but honestly, friend, I believe those were His exact words. That's all He said, but somehow I knew exactly what He meant: <u>cigarettes.</u>

It was as if I had put up a wall of smoke between myself and my creator God! I knew that wall had to come down no matter what the cost!

While still on my knees, I began to reflect on the real meaning of the gospel—the amazing love and compassion of God! And how on that terrible day at Calvary, He demonstrated His love for us while we were still sinners! I thought about the awful pain and suffering that Jesus went through as He hung on the cross to pay for our sins and cleanse us from all unrighteousness…so that we may escape the torments of hell and live in heaven forever with Him. Also I reflected on Jesus crying out from the cross, *"Father forgive them, for they know not what they do."* And now, I hear God telling me to <u>clean up my act</u>. I shouldn't be surprised. The first thing Jesus said when He began to preach was *"Repent, for the kingdom of God is at hand."* (Matthew 4:17)

Then I thought about how little pain I would suffer by comparison when I try to kick the tobacco habit. Do I love my Savior enough to withstand a little pain for His sake? Yes I do! So I pray once more, "God, I don't care if it kills me, <u>I promise you</u>: I will never again put a cigarette in my mouth as long as I live." AMEN!

God knew that I meant business! What a blessing followed! The wall of sin that had separated me from God was blown away. This time, it was no problem to kick the habit—no headaches, no withdrawal pains, no more vacillation, no stress! I kept the promise. I felt God's *peace that passes all understanding* and His presence once again, just as I did 35 years prior when I first called out to God, "Oh God, if you are real, please take control of my life!"

He heard my prayer and I was gloriously born again by His Spirit. (John 3:3) Now I understand what it means to be "in Christ." It's the same as having the <u>Spirit of Christ living in you.</u> You can read much about this wonderful work of the Holy Spirit in Romans chapter eight.

Of all the miracles that Jesus ever did, the greatest miracle of all can happen today for <u>you</u> if you have never been born again. When you are <u>willing</u> to admit that that you are a sinner—and open your heart in prayer to receive the Holy Spirit—Jesus forgives all your past sins and comes in and gives you a new life—with power to break the chains of addiction to any habit that will destroy your happiness—and power to live a life that is pleasing to God!

How can this be? And why am I sharing this with you? When God created man in His own image, He gave him an organ called the human spirit. This is the organ that God designed to be filled with His Spirit. II Corinthians: 5-17 states *"If any man be in Christ , he is a new creation . ."* All the miracles that Jesus did when He walked the earth were for this reason: to teach us to trust Him and give Him control of our lives; and allow us to receive the greatest miracle of all—new birth *in Christ.* Remember, Jesus said *"Seek and you shall find. Ask and you shall receive."*

Now because God loves you with an everlasting love, the Christ in me loves you too. I'm praying that as you read this, God will give you the faith to believe that Jesus Christ is Lord... that He loves you more than you'll ever know... and what He did for a rotten sinner like me, He can also do for you!

If you would like to talk to me about this, give me a call at (888) 779-4280, and perhaps we can get together. I will try to help you any way that I can. One thing I can do is to help you find a church that teaches the Holy Bible and help you learn how you can enjoy all of God's precious promises!

Sincerely,
G. Warren Sears

Appendix 2.

A talk at the Toastmasters Club

WHAT MAKES A GREAT COMMUNICATOR?

I have pondered that question many times, and I am thankful that the things we are learning here with Toastmasters is very helpful. However, if we really wish to excel at communication, I believe we could all profit by studying the words and the life of the greatest communicator that ever lived.

As He said, "Heaven and earth shall pass away, but my words shall not pass away." Of course, I'm talking about Jesus. If you've never done so, I would like to encourage you to read the New Testament and ask yourself, "How can it be that the words of Jesus have made such an impact on the world?" How can it be that the words He spoke nearly 2000 years ago are still changing people's lives and the course of History?

For example, in the summer of 1999, I met a man who told me a remarkable story. He came from the northern most part of Burma. One hundred years ago, it was the most primitive country you could imagine. A tropical climate existed the year round and the natives never wore clothes. Although they had no education, they were never idol worshipers. As they studied the stars, they were intelligent enough to understand—there had to be a creator God in control.

So when a Christian missionary couple from America went there to tell them about God, they gladly welcomed them. The Burmese people had no written language. So first they taught them the alphabet, made a dictionary and spent 75 years there translating the whole Bible into their language and taught them how to read it. Today, 95% of the people there are Christians. The man who told me the story came to Washington, DC here as a missionary and is now pastoring a Burmese Christian church in Chinatown, DC.

I offer you these examples of Jesus and the missionaries to dramatize one aspect of successful communication: they had credibility. They addressed the needs of the people. They both sacrificially demonstrated their love for them. Therefore, the people trusted them and believed that they spoke the truth.

You and I could learn to deliver a speech with all the skills of a graduate Toastmaster, but if we have earned a reputation for lying, if we have no credibility—our words will fall on deaf ears.

In closing, I encourage you to read the Holy Bible. You will see that Jesus spoke boldly, with authority, and you will enjoy His many illustrations. Not only is it the greatest example of communication ever written, it is God's final message to us before He appears again in person.

For those of you who do not believe the Bible is reliable, please consider this fact: There are more than 300 prophecies in the Old Testament written hundreds of years in advance concerning the important events in the Life of Jesus that were all fulfilled in exact detail in the New Testament. Jesus told His disciples that He must go to Jerusalem where He would be mocked, spitted upon, scourged, and killed. But after 3 days, He would rise again.

What do you suppose would have become of His disciples if they had not seen the risen Christ on the third day after His burial? If I were in that boat, I would have come to the conclusion that Jesus was either a liar or a lunatic and I would have soon gone back to fishing. But hallelujah, they all saw the risen Savior, and they even had a picnic with Him by the Sea of Galilee... and when they were given power from above, in spite of persecution, they spent the rest of their lives communicating His story.

And His story is now HISTORY!

Appendix 3

BOOKS ABOUT CREATION VS. EVOLUTION—

Icons of Evolution—Science or Myth? by Jonathan Wells

Body By Design by Alan A. Gillen

Defeating Darwinism by Opening Minds; Darwin on Trial; and *Reason in the Balance* by Phillip E. Johnson

Appendix 4

HOW TO FIND A GOOD CHURCH

As the Bible predicted, we are now living in the age of apostasy—the time when many churches no longer preach and teach the truth according to God's Word. Many churches today have large congregations, yet they are only social clubs! They may have a beautiful building with a steeple and a cross pointing to the heavens; yet as in Revelation 3:20, Christ may be on the outside knocking on the door, but no one opens the door to let Him in.

If you want your life to please God, you must belong to a church that is right in God's eyes. So then, how can you make the right choice?

This is my advice. Simply visit the pastor, or phone, and ask him these questions:

1/ Do you believe and teach that the whole Bible is the Word of God AND should not be added to or taken away from? *(Rev. 22:18-19)*

2/ Is Jesus the only begotten Son of God? *(John 3:16)*

3/ Was Jesus supernaturally conceived by the Holy Spirit and born of a virgin? *(Isaiah 7:14)*

4/ Did Jesus die on the cross to pay for our sins, and rise again on the third day? *(I Corinthians 15: 3-19)*

5/ Are we saved by faith alone, or does salvation depend upon our good works? *(Ephesians 2:8-9)*

6/ Is Jesus literally coming back to earth to catch up believers in the air? *(I Thessalonians 4:15-18)*

7/ Is faith in Christ the only way to receive the gift of eternal life? *(John 14:6)*

8/ Do you believe that God created us in His image according to Genesis One (as opposed to Darwinism)? *(Genesis 1:26)*

9/ Is it improper for a woman to pastor a church? *(I Timothy 2:12-14)*

If the Pastor does not answer yes to all of these questions, look for another church.

Getting involved in a good church will help you and encourage you to grow spiritually. Hebrews 10:24 says, *Not forsaking the assembling of ourselves together, as the manner of some is, but exhorting one another as you see the day (judgment day) approaching."*

God loves you the way you are, but he is not willing for you to stay that way. *(Romans 8:28-29)*

Appendix 5.

ACROSTIC REMINDER OF FOUR BASIC STEPS TO SHARE THE GOSPEL

F FIRST—pray for power of Holy Spirit.

I INQUIRE about person's spiritual beliefs.

S SHARE my personal salvation experience.

H HEAVEN or hell. Receive the gift or…

Appendix 6.

SUGGESTED READING

Evangelism Explosion. By D. James Kennedy

What If Jesus Had Never Been Born? By D. James Kennedy

The Gospel According To Jesus. By John MacArthur

Sharing Jesus Without Fear. By Bill Fay

How To Give Away Your Faith. By Paul E. Little

Becoming a Contagious Christian. By Paul Hybels and Mark Mittleburg

Witnessing To Jews. By Moise and Ceil Rosen

Witnessing Without Fear. By Bill Bright

The Master Plan of Evangelism. By Robert Coleman

Experiencing God: Knowing and Doing The Will of God.
By Henry T. Blackaby and Claude V. King

My Utmost For His Highest. By Oswald Chambers

The Case for Christ. By Lee Strobel

Left Behind. By Tim Lahaye and Jerry Jenkins

God's Best for My Life. By Lloyd John Ogilvie

Questioning Evangelism. By Randy Newman

*Answers to Tough Questions Skeptics Ask About the
Christian Faith.* By Josh McDowell and Don Stewart

*Show and Then Tell: Presenting the Gospel Through Daily
Encounters.* By Kent and Davidene Humphreys

Appendix 7.

EXERCISE YOUR IMAGINATION

What could you say to: an accountant, a waiter, a printer, a
writer, an artist, a farmer, a lawyer, a doctor, a builder, a
fisherman, a prostitute, a dope pusher, a salesman, a cook, a
musician, a stone mason, a brick layer, a cleaning person, a
soldier, an airplane pilot, a sign painter, a landscape designer,
a nurse, a topless dancer, a senator, an actor, a baker, a model,
a photographer, a clerk, a carpenter, or a gardener?

Pray about an interesting and a positive way to engage them
in conversation by relating their vocation or interests to the
Lord Jesus. This can be very useful as well as fun.

Appendix 8.

OVERCOMING FEARS, AND OTHER EXCUSES FOR NOT WITNESSING

Fear of offending people.

That is one of the excuses for not witnessing that I hear most often. I understand. I've been there too. But one day the Lord gave me a little glimpse of reality that made that excuse look awfully limp—I envisioned someone waking up in hell—screaming with horrible pain! I imagined the awful stench of smoke and burning flesh. He was one of those 'nice guys' who had once been a friend of mine—but I, being afraid of offending him, had never once warned him of the eternal consequences of his sin of unbelief.

I wonder how offended he felt towards me on the day he woke up and found himself in the lake of fire? Think about that the next time God gives you a chance to talk to your unsaved friends and acquaintances. It may be your last chance. You could start by sharing John 3:16. No one gets offended for telling them that God loves them. But don't forget to share verses 17 and 18.

Fear of not knowing enough.

The gospel is so simple even a child can understand it. I have met people that were saved when they were only three years old. It is simply the good news that Jesus died to take the punishment for our sins, was buried and after three days He rose again.

An effective way to share the gospel from the Bible is to take them through a short series of scripture verses—often called the "Roman's Road." (My utmost thanks to William Fay for his great book entitled, "Share Jesus Without Fear" where he suggests the following easy way to do this.) *Note the page number of Romans 3:23 in the front of your*

Bible, then highlight that verse. Then, in the margin, make a small note of the next page number to turn to and highlight Rom. 6:23. Do the same thing with each succeeding verse: John 3:3, John 14:6, Rom. 10:9-11, 2 Cor. 5:15, and Rev. 3:20.

William Fay's book further suggests... *ask the person to read each verse aloud, and then ask, "What does this verse say to you?" If they don't get it right, just ask them to please read it aloud again. Continue doing this with each succeeding verse until they can tell you what it means.*

Quite often, as they read the word of God aloud, the Holy Spirit will convict them and they will be ready to pray the sinner's prayer and receive Christ as Lord and Savior.

Of course, Fay's book has many more details about using his method—and I seriously encourage every Christian to order this book from your local Christian book store.

Fear of rejection.

Unredeemed sinners have rejected God, so naturally they will reject us when we preach to them. We can expect that to happen. But that is not something we need to fear. *"For God has not given us the spirit of fear, but of power, and of love, and of a sound mind."* (II Timothy 1:7)

We must pray for boldness even as Paul did. And thank God for His gift of power, love, and a sound mind as we stay in His presence through prayer.

Sometimes we need to ask ourselves the question: "What is most important—to please men or to please God?" I believe one of the saddest statements in the Bible is a prophesy of Isaiah in John 12:42-43: *"...among the chief rulers also many believed on Him (Jesus); but because of the Pharisees they did not confess Him, lest they should be put out of the synagogue; For they loved the praise of men more than the praise of God."*

I don't have the gift of evangelism.

That may be true, because that is one of the spiritual gifts that God gives to whom He chooses. Yet according to Acts 1:8, we <u>all</u> are given power by the Holy Spirit to be witnesses. And according to II Corinthians 5:17-20, we <u>all</u> are called to be ambassadors for Christ.

I am physically handicapped.

Pray for God to show you how you can be a witness by telephoning or writing letters to unsaved friends and relatives. After all, most of the New Testament is simply a collection of personal letters... and Paul wrote Phillipians while he was in prison.

For a present-day example of a handicapped person whom the Lord uses in a mighty way, read the wonderful story of Joni Erikson Tada. Joni became a paraplegic as a result of a diving accident in her teens, and she spends most of her life in a wheel chair. In spite of that, she has a regular national radio broadcast, and designs beautiful Christian greeting cards by holding brushes and color pencils in her mouth.

I don't have enough time.

Is there any activity in your life that perhaps could be adjusted in order to gain time? How about some of the time you spend watching TV; shopping for worldly treasures; surfing the net; looking for entertainment; or reading newspapers? We must pray for wisdom concerning this.

A college professor said recently, "I only spend 15 minutes a day reading newspapers. All the stories are the same. They just have different names and different places.

I realized recently that reading junk mail and charity solicitations was wasting too much of my time, so I came up with this solution: I mailed a letter to all the charities I wish to support, saying: "Instead of mailing donations every month, I am sending you a <u>one-time annual donation</u> for the year. PLEASE SAVE OUR TIME, PAPER AND MAILING COSTS by <u>removing my name from your mail list</u> for the remainder of this year.

*   *   *

What do you say to a POLICEMAN?

I appreciate you men. You have probably risked your life many times to protect innocent people and keep the peace. Do you know that Jesus said "Blessed are the peacemakers. They shall be called the children of God." He was talking about helping people to have peace with God. Jesus called it being born again—born from above. And he said, "except you are born again you cannot see the kingdom of God" Can I show you in the Bible what that means?

AUDIO BOOKS
will soon be available

For information, phone me
toll-free at (888) 779-4280
or e-mail me at Gwarrensears@aol.com

Did you enjoy this book?

Then please tell: your pastor, assistant pastor, youth pastor, ministry leader, evangelism director, and talk-radio host.

Warren welcomes all opportunities to speak to your church, group, event, retreat… or wherever saints gather.

He teaches, motivates, and encourages all Christians to be fearless, effective, and joyful witnesses for our wonderful Lord Jesus.

And, *upon request,* he loves to glorify God with a solo on his sanctified saxophone.

HAVE BOOKS
HAVE SAX
WILL TRAVEL

Let's talk. Phone:

G. Warren Sears

(888) 779-4280

(toll-free)

Gwarrensears@aol.com

"And the things that thou hast heard from me among many witnesses, the same commit thou to faithful men, who shall be able to teach others also."

2 TIMOTHY 2:2

BOOK ORDER FORM

The easiest way to order more books
is directly from the publisher.

By telephone: TOLL FREE
(866) 8333-YAV {833-3928}

On the Internet
www.InterestingWriting.com

By mail, complete form and mail to:
YAV Publications
122 Greenmeadow Dr.
Timonium, MD 21093

Please send the number of copies indicated on the form below to:

Name _____

Address _____

City _____ State _____ Zip _____

My personal check is enclosed for _____ # of books, or charge my

Credit card. (circle one) Visa   Master Card   American Express   Discover

Card number _____ Exp. date _____

Name on card _____

First copy: $13.80 ($10.95 plus $2.85 shipping and handling)
Each additional copy: $11.95 ($10.95 plus $1.00 S & H)
FREE SHIPPING for 20 books or more

Bookstores: Please order from Ingram

CPSIA information can be obtained at www.ICGtesting.com
Printed in the USA
BVOW04s2119310315

394156BV00007B/74/P